Carl,

During the fall of 1960 two events occurred that were to have a profound effect upon a senior bent on pursuing a football coaching career.

One was the presidential campaign and victory of a young, dynamic politician whose beliefs and life-style were to sweep up this senior in the emotions of an entirely new and wonderful experience.

The second event was the arrival on the MSC campus of a young instructor from Pitt. During countless evenings in the nine months that followed, a rather politically-naive student sat in awe as the instructor discoursed over a wide range of topics from the world of politics and political science.

This book, I trust, is one way of reminding you how much that academic year 1960-61 meant to me.

In January I accepted a position, effective this fall, as assistant professor of political science at the Ohio State University in Columbus.

Jim Harf

The Kennedy Literature

THE KENNEDY LITERATURE:
A Bibliographical Essay on
John F. Kennedy

by James Tracy Crown

New York: New York University Press
London: University of London Press Limited
1968

© 1968 by New York University
Library of Congress Catalog Card Number: 68—29428
Manufactured in the United States of America
Design by James Mafchir

Contents

	An Introductory Essay	3
Chapter I	Kennedy's Writing	51
Chapter II	The Major Biographies	75
Chapter III	Personal Material, Including Kennedy's Growth, Family, and His Circle	83
Chapter IV	Campaigns	93
Chapter V	Presidency: Actions, Policies, Politics, Administration, Associated Personalities	101
Chapter VI	Relations With Groups of Citizens	123
Chapter VII	Critics: Gentle and Severe	127
Chapter VIII	The Assassination: The Warren Commission, Doubts, and Alternative Explanations	143
Chapter IX	Further Research and the Kennedy Library	169
	Index	175
	Biographical Note on James Tracy Crown	183

Foreword

Five years after John Kennedy's death we are beginning to put his life and his Presidency into some kind of perspective. This is not because history renders a verdict—at best history renders only a series of verdicts—but because the perceptions and memories of historians and journalists, of politicians and people, are as crucial in forming that perspective as the "actual facts" themselves. And rarely has a man attracted so much writing before, during, and after his Presidency as did Kennedy.

Too, the books about the late President were published so quickly and abundantly that they became very much part of the Kennedy era. Hence Professor Crown's volume is far more than a selective bibliography; it is a long commentary on Kennedy as both the maker and subject of history. This interplay is strikingly reflected in Professor Crown's exhaustive list of Kennedy's own writings—along with a fascinating roundup of the charges that the writings were mainly ghostwritten.

Professor Crown made a calculated choice in favor of critical commentaries on a selective list of writings about Kennedy rather than a complete bibliography. One result is the omission of some admirable contemporary volumes such as Helen Fuller's *Year of Trial* or Stan Opotowski's *The Kennedy Government*. He also decided to omit most of the numerous picture books on Kennedy, including, unfortunately, Joan Meyers (ed.), *John Fitzgerald Kennedy As We Remember Him*, a superb collection of interviews, documents, and pictures and in my view (a highly subjective one, in part because I wrote a concluding essay) the most evocative portrait of Kennedy that we have.

Still, I prefer the shorter list with Professor Crown's extended and knowledgeable commentaries. Some will disagree with his evaluations, especially with his rather generous treatment of some of the Kennedy biographers. In my own case, it is possible that by leaning over to be "objective" about John Kennedy I did not fully gauge the quickening pace of personal fulfillment that would ultimately produce a great man in the White House. But if none of us has produced a biography quite worthy of the many-faceted man and his turbulent era, at least Professor Crown implies a standard for later biographers to aspire to.

All Presidents—indeed all effective politicians—are supersensitive to what the press says about them; Kennedy was no exception. But I know of no recent President, save Franklin Roosevelt, who was as concerned as Kennedy about what history would say of him. Was he simply fortunate, or also calculating, that two of his aides would turn out to be effective chroniclers of his days in the White House? Kennedy was intensely concerned with the question of how future generations would regard him; as a political scientist Professor Crown would doubtless agree that while future historians will comprise a shifting, prickly, and contrary lot, there are worse constituencies for a President to feel accountable to.

James MacGregor Burns

The Kennedy Literature

An Introductory Essay

THE CONTINUING INTEREST IN THE KENNEDY LITERATURE

"You be Kennedy and I'll be Spivak," Senator John F. Kennedy told a guest on an afternoon before he was to appear on Lawrence Spivak's TV program, "Meet the Press." Kennedy continued as "Spivak": "All right, Horatio Alger, just what makes you think you want to be President?"

This Kennedy game, described in Benjamin Bradlee's book *That Special Grace,* tells us a great deal about Kennedy's wit. It also demonstrates that Kennedy was well aware that his meteoric career elicited admiration as well as resentment, hope as well as skepticism. In asking why there is such sustained fascination with the Kennedy literature, part of the answer is to be found in the way people continue to explore whether Kennedy was merely a Golden Boy whom Americans envied and admired, or, instead, a strong leader whose solid accomplishments can be measured by standards applied to less legendary men. This question runs like an elusive thread through most of the Kennedy literature. More than one reader has changed his mind on the question midway through a heavy volume only to change it again when concluding a slim, tightly reasoned essay—only to go on reading.

It is easy to see why this hesitation about Kennedy's rank among Presidents occurs. Theodore Sorensen presents Kennedy as a great man, and supports his claim with an appendix listing Kennedy's legislative achievements and the likely prospects for other Kennedy measures. Too many critics slight Kennedy the achiever without acknowledging these hard facts. Allied with his former colleague Sorensen, Arthur Schlesinger, Jr., says Kennedy had a splendid mind and shrewd grasp of politics. On the contrary, Norman Mailer predicts that despite Kennedy's "existential charm," historically he would probably be outranked by Fidel Castro. Malcolm Muggeridge finds Kennedy unbelievably banal. Henry Fairlie is insufferably bored by Kennedy. Sam Rayburn, William Carleton, Arthur Krock, and Roger Hagan seem to damn Kennedy with faint praise. Yet, varied as these views are, each should be read by those who want to know what Kennedy was like, as well as how his Administration appeared to contemporaries. An interesting Kennedy quality, incidentally, is revealed in the writing or recorded conversation of some of his severest critics. It was common even for them to like Kennedy despite their reservations and to attempt in their minds a fair appraisal of him. Most of those who really hated him and were blinded by their hatred either couldn't or didn't take pen in hand. The man with whom Kennedy fought a sometimes comic, sometimes tragic duel throughout his Presidential life said, upon hearing of his assassination, "Es una mala noticia." Two and a half years later, Fidel Castro added; "Johnson is a mediocre bandit, where Kennedy was an intelligent bandit, though they both serve the same interests . . . Kennedy was a personality of value . . ."

Although their needs fall into more numerous specific categories, as indicated below, there are two general groups of readers who have the strongest continuing interest in the Kennedy literature. The author of this bibliography has kept in mind their different backgrounds and needs. For the first group the Kennedy story in its various aspects is very much a part of their living memory. There is already a younger second group, however, for whom John F. Kennedy is someone they have only heard of and about whose death they know more than his life.

Those already steeped in the Kennedy lore will turn to the Kennedy literature mainly to clarify aspects of the young President's life which remain unexplored, inadequately explained, or challenged. They are curious to know whether the chroniclers of the man and his brief period paint a picture as they remember it and saw it. They will not settle for televised accounts, for they have in mind something akin to the pretelevision, but pertinent admonition of poet William Blake who warned: "They ever will believe a lie; Who see with, not through the eye." They know they will find deep analysis only in the printed word, but they also know that the significance of events also can be lost through trivialization—a current literary style which stuns the reader with a flood of undigested details but quite befogs meaning. Such readers of a bibliography seek to separate the relevant from the irrelevant.

Some readers who lived the Kennedy days approach a critical and objective bibliography with difficulty. They may feel some reluctance to leave a man for whom they feel affection to the dissections of the historian and bibliographer. They are somewhat leery of what they consider to be "literary cormorants" and they may agree with Voltaire's contention that "History is, after all, only a bag of tricks we play on the dead." For most of them, however, who trouble to turn to a bibliography, the sense of intellectual inquiry will overcome this understandable reserve, and they will conclude, with biographer Samuel Johnson, that it is better to know the facts and opinions about a man than not to know. They may also recall that this was John F. Kennedy's approach in reading biography. He also recognized that, by and large, the life of a public man was of public interest and he even had a zest for the small change of social life.

The younger major group of readers will have the dispassionate advantage of approaching John F. Kennedy as a purely historic figure. They will have less difficulty with objectivity but more need of annotation. Despite modern communication, political awareness, much less concern, does not always come early to the young. Five years after the death of a Woodrow Wilson, Franklin Roosevelt, or a John Kennedy, students enter high school and even college with minimal consciousness of these figures who dominated the political talk of their elders. Yet such students are frequently motivated to sort through presidential literature in order to find out why their father or professor was so excitedly for or against a figure who was, for them, a special president.

A major purpose of this work, then, is to select and comment upon the Kennedy Literature in a way which will be useful and interesting

6 THE KENNEDY LITERATURE

to both those who have a considerable background in the subject as well as those who approach this writing afresh.

THE USES OF THIS BIBLIOGRAPHY

This bibliography is designed to be useful both to the general reader who seeks to distinguish the relevant from the irrelevant and quality from dross, but more particularly it is designed for the researcher, whether of a term paper or thesis, article or book, who delves deeply into a chosen aspect of John F. Kennedy's life or actions.

Often the general reader, whether scholarly or not, wishes either consciously or unconsciously, to put himself vicariously in the shoes of the subject studied. He will be interested in the major biographies and biographical sketches, and may seek to know what can be learned about human nature, and what is the vision of the good life held by a gifted person in mid-twentieth-century America, as well as what combination of attributes are to be found in an unusual man who captures the imagination of intellectuals and more ordinary people alike. Others will wish to learn what Kennedy wrote and taught, for he was very much and very consciously a popular teacher.

Through selective reading the general reader can also find interest in tracing the development of mind, character, and career. He can probe for motivation beneath the usual shibboleths and encomiums. It can be a stimulating pursuit for them as it was for the popular historian, Kennedy himself, who found that in the case of each man he wrote about "complexities, inconsistencies and doubts arise to plague us." Motivation, he wrote, in *Profiles in Courage,* "is always difficult to assess. It is particularly difficult to trace in the murky sea of politics."

Closely allied with his motivation are his political intentions which, in Kennedy's case, are more elaborately set forth in writing than is true of any twentieth-century presidential candidate except Woodrow Wilson. This opens the way to an enlightening comparison of a young candidate's hopes and aspirations with forces and limitations he encountered once in office.

The larger significance of this is the light the example of Kennedy's Presidency sheds on a great debate currently taking place among serious students of the Presidency. One school of thought holds that the

President, in his constitutional position and in practice, is able to be almost as powerful a democratic leader as his desires and his skills allow. Another current view of the office is that like the rest of American national government, the Presidency is pretty much a holding operation. In fact, it is argued for this view, Americans have invented the myth of the great presidents in order to excuse the inability of other parts of the federal system to solve basic national problems. These presidents, this argument runs, are remembered more for what they said, rather than for what they did; even their achievements are mainly negative—as in the military field—rather than positive. Shocking as this view may be to a generation educated to look upon the Presidency as the focal point of the world's most effective government, it is a view which, with modification, is receiving increasingly serious consideration—with the disputed record of the Kennedy Administration becoming one of the centers of contention. The entries concerning Kennedy's Presidency will be of central concern to those interested in this question.

Other general readers may wish to know primarily what were Kennedy's relations with his brothers and family, or with such important political blocks as business, unions, Catholics, Negroes, and intellectuals. Others seem determined to skip over the life of this graceful man to the grislier world of "Dallasology" and contention over who was responsible for the assassination and what are the political implications. Some, pursuing the gentle American art of "debunking" will seek out titles which help toward that end. All such readers, as the Table of Contents indicates, will find headings for categories of special interest to them.

Both general readers and scholarly researchers, it is assumed, want bibliographical entries not only to distinguish the relevant from the irrelevant, but where appropriate to comment as well on the entries' accuracy, completeness and critical soundness. Under each category, entries are listed as far as possible chronologically. It is assumed also that readers want frank evaluations as long as they are fair-minded. Toward this end, for example, annotations indicate what in terms of first hand information is the best biography, what is the most gracefully written book, what is the worst article ever written on Kennedy, why many serious readers find it difficult to believe completely in either the Warren Commission's *Report* or in any single work of its critics. It is also assumed that bibliographies need not be dull affairs, but rather in the discussion of relevant works may capture some of the flavor hidden beneath the titles.

While many of these bibliographical qualities serve any kind of reader, this bibliography, as has been indicated, will probably best serve the researcher whether he is an undergraduate writing a term paper, or a Ph.D. scholar wishing to analyze the basic evidence. Students of history, political science, American studies, journalism, and communications, who wish to explore such topics as the psychology of leadership, the history of ideas, and the "Hero" in nonfiction will all, hopefully, find this book most useful.

Kennedy once spent a college year reading the record of a little-known Republican congressman. "The thought that some zealous and critical sophomore is now dissecting my own record in a similar class often causes me some concern," he wrote years later. Of course, as he half hoped, some zealous sophomore *is* doing exactly that. The flood of information has really, however, only provided the groundwork from which serious analysis may now begin in earnest.

In the author's work with the Kennedy literature and directing student research a number of topics have suggested themselves which can be undertaken by using appropriate listed titles plus the index to major works as well as the index of this bibliography. Among them are: The Sociology of the Kennedy Family; Change and Continuity in the Ideas of John F. Kennedy; Kennedy's Political Use of the "Missile Gap" Charge; Kennedy's Administrative Ideas; The Decline of the Catholic Issue During the Kennedy Presidency; Kennedy as a Symbol of Changing American Taste and Style; Television in Kennedy's Political Career; The Republican View of the Kennedy Campaign; The Question of the Competence of Kennedy's Legislative Staff; The Political Triangle of JFK, RFK, and LBJ; Kennedy's Concept of the Balance of Power; Why almost Half the Electorate Voted for Nixon in 1960; and Johnson's Claim of Continuing the Kennedy Policy in Vietnam.

One limitation on the scope of this bibliography should be mentioned before concluding this discussion of its uses. Because of the need for focus and coherence in the Kennedy literature, this bibliography does not treat works by or about his successor, President Lyndon B. Johnson, except as his career as Senator and Vice President was relevant and where comparisons which have been made between their two administrations casts interesting or important light on the administration of John F. Kennedy. Likewise books and articles about Robert F. Kennedy, himself a growing subject of literature, are treated only as he was involved in the career of his older brother or where the style and legend of John F. Kennedy seem to have affected Robert's career and American political style in general.

TOOLS FOR CRITICAL EVALUATION

The writers I have selected do the student the greatest service when they provide him with a provocative hypothesis—a serious, though tentative statement—which he can test for himself. The more provocative the hypothesis, the more firmly held will be the student's conclusion. In scholarship, as in motoring, the most dangerous place is often the middle of the road. Let us examine, then, some of the possible hypotheses offered by different authors in this bibliography.

One hypothesis is that Kennedy was basically incompetent in handling power relationships; a second, that Kennedy was one of the master politicians of the last half century; a third, that Kennedy's career was cut short before any decision on the first two hypotheses could be made either way. Other conflicting hypotheses, for which I have had equally convincing term papers submitted, are: (1) that the outcome of the Cuban missile crisis was an unqualified triumph for Kennedy and the United States; and (2) that the Soviets basically gained more from the Cuban missile crisis than did the United States.

In trying to reach a definite conclusion from a working hypothesis, the reader should bear some questions in mind while evaluating the material cited in this bibliography and determining a writer's reliability. First, is the report firsthand? Second, is the book or article written soon after the event occurred or much later? A writer's memory of events and conversations (though not necessarily his perspective or writing style) is better when closer to the event—Schlesinger, Sorensen, and Evelyn Lincoln were wise to write promptly. Thus, to aid the student in determining the chronology of the entries within each section, entries are arranged as much as possible in order of their date of publication.

A third question the reader should ask is whether a writer's work on Kennedy is intended to justify that writer's participation in the event discussed; quite often, a disinterested outsider's analysis is more reliable for the reader than that of a committed insider. "Every great man nowadays has his disciples," wrote Charles Feuss, "and it is always Judas who writes the biography." This was not so in the case of Kennedy—the closest men around him were all his unashamed partisans. Even critics whose intellectual attitude toward Presidents of the past had been "You can't criticize unresisting imbecility," frequently took sustenance from berating Kennedy because they thought he just might hear them, and, in any event, they knew he regarded ideas as important in politics.

The prospective researcher should remember there are different kinds of journalists. Those who have the time and a sharp mentality are every bit as good as scholars, and journalists frequently ask the right questions—William Shannon and Joseph Kraft come readily to mind. Sometimes, when the journalists are too Establishment-oriented for their own good, a young scholar such as Edward Jay Epstein will embarrass them. However, on the whole, the works in the scholarly journals or dissertations do not contribute impressively to the Kennedy literature, and this is due more to a failure to ask meaningful questions than to the immediacy of the subject.

Unfortunately, enemies of the modern biography are the telephone, which Kennedy used to conduct a good deal of his business, and the conference at which *aide mémoires* are not kept. When either of these two sources is quoted directly, the reader should exercise reservations.

A further complication, as Kennedy's advisers readily admit, is that Kennedy never revealed everything he was doing to any one person. He liked to quote de Maistre's advice that in "all political systems, there are relationships which it is wise to leave undefined." Accordingly, the young President commonly gave two or more persons the same assignment unbeknown to each other. This compartmentalization of information permitted Kennedy to keep all the cards in his own hand. It also explains why writers "in the know" (or so they assumed) came up with completely different, though perfectly honest, versions of the same event.

Finally, the researchers should exercise the greatest caution when comparing different views of Kennedy's family relationships. In biography, as in fiction, this area is always most difficult to penetrate illuminatingly and convincingly. With his family as with his administrative aides, Kennedy's method of using information must be kept in mind. It cannot safely be assumed that even his wife or brothers knew always and precisely what he had in mind. Interviews with them are too seldom read with awareness of this.

For those interested further in the problems of determining reliability and truth in the process of scholarship, a reading of John A. Garraty's *The Nature of Biography* is highly recommended. In it he discusses, among other things, the scientific problem of memory and evidence. Harold D. Lasswell's *Power and Personality* explores many points pertinent to the Kennedy literature, adds perspective, and suggests useful lines of approach to such a subject.

THE ALL-OUT SKEPTICS

What does the Kennedy literature offer to those whose skepticism is almost absolute, and who simply refuse to believe anything about a man who had a huge public relations machine and who held office during a period when "national security" was so often indiscriminately invoked? As one skeptic grumbled, "An Administration which can turn the rocking chair into a vitality symbol can do anything with images." Such skeptics know that when a family accumulates as much money as the Kennedys, it commonly hires someone to keep any of the family's awkward goings-on out of the newspapers. This negative side of public relations, skeptics argue, can be as misleading as the artificial generation of news, and they cite instances in the Kennedy literature where Joseph Kennedy intervened with publishers in his son's behalf to suppress potentially damaging information. Indeed, Sorensen admits one of his most unpleasant tasks was to chastize writers on the President's instructions. He denies, however, the widely credited reports that errant reporters lost their jobs upon losing their White House access, but admits that "we talked more freely and more frequently with our friends." The skeptic will hardly be convinced by Sorensen's interpretation that in his early months in the White House, Kennedy's "chastisements of newsmen for stories he felt were unfair or inaccurate . . . unfortunately led to charges that he was not only oversensitive to unfavorable stories, which he was, but also attempting to intimidate the author's thinking, which he was not."

In 1958, Sorensen notes, Kennedy "waged an intensive effort with his contacts in the publishing world to prevent a projected biography by a writer inaccurately representing himself as a Kennedy intimate." Sorensen's only excuse for this, in Kennedy's behalf, was that Kennedy considered the writer "uninformed, unobjective and unsound"— hardly faults which remove the First Amendment guarantees. So responsible (if partisan) a figure as Governor Nelson Rockefeller of New York charged that Kennedy critic Victor Lasky was being investigated by Robert Kennedy's Justice Department as a result of his book lambasting President Kennedy.

As indicated in an annotated selection which follows, Senator Kennedy, while on a campaign trip to Oregon, took time out to phone a Boston writer, Joseph Dinneen, and successfully insist that he delete from his manuscript of *The Kennedy Family* an interview with Joseph P. Kennedy on the subject of anti-Semitism.

The attempts of Kennedy, his family, or his associates to affect the content or even the very life of books relating to them did not cease upon the President's death. The Manchester episode tested in glaring public view the varied Kennedy family, author, and public interpretations of a reader's right to know, the right to privacy, and the relation of political convenience to an author's interpretation of truth. Skepticism was fed by the results of this controversy as well as by Kennedy family attempts to make this version of the assassination, a version over which Mrs. Kennedy and Senator Robert Kennedy had by contract special influence, the sole nonofficial, detailed version of the tragedy. Reports such as Drew Pearson's "Jackie's Crackdown on the JFK Books," *New York Post,* September 6, 1966, were also widely read. Later Professor Murray B. Levin who had written a book about the 1962 Senate campaign of the President's brother Edward Kennedy complained in *Books,* October, 1966, p. 6, that the Kennedy's had successfully put pressure on a number of publishers causing them to turn down his book which was finally published by Beacon Press.

Later, the handling of the Robert Baker investigation also fed doubts about the ability of readers to get the full story subsequent to Kennedy's death concerning important aspects of the Kennedy Administration. The Baker disclosures affected not only the reputation of the Kennedy Administration for keeping high standards in Washington but also the political future of Kennedy's Vice President. Not only did the Senate Rules Committee's investigation seem to impartial observers to be very partisan, but the White House, by then in President Johnson's charge, intervened in the case in a manner not soon to be forgotten by skeptics. In a story entitled "Witness Assailed by Johnson Aides," *New York Times,* February 8, 1964, the *Times* recounted several instances of White House attempts to discredit a witness who had linked Robert Baker and Johnson in an unsavory business way. "In a third instance," the *Times* reported, "the publisher of a national news magazine was called by long-distance telephone by someone described to the *Times* as 'an important White House personage, but not the President.' There was more than one telephone call in this instance, in which the caller 'warned' the publisher that any article based on Reynold's testimony would probably be inaccurate. Excerpts allegedly from F.B.I. files were read to the publisher to substantiate the 'warning.' " The possibility that the White House staff, during the administration of Kennedy's successor, would feel free to attempt to alter, delay, or suppress a news story by employing F.B.I. files to impune the character of a witness must be taken into consideration in assessing the pressures under which writers work in attempting to carry out their responsibility of free reporting.

Of course Kennedy and his Administration had no direct responsibility for this, even though the practices of subsequent administrations can affect our ability to gain a clear picture of the Kennedy Administration. Furthermore, skeptics believe that the "credibility gap" which became notorious during the Johnson Administration had at least some of its roots in the "news management" practices of the Kennedy Administration.

There are other, earlier instances of tampering with political news. Sorensen himself admits he attributed authorship of his own memorandum on Catholic voting to others so it would be more convincing to the press (the press swallowed this version whole). Malcolm Muggeridge in reviewing Sorensen's book insists that some Kennedy intimates privately speak of an amorous, indolent, and snobbish aspect of Kennedy which is not present in works about him, although these intimates often include excessive details on other matters.

Arthur Schlesinger, Jr., too, became involved in charges of Kennedy Administration deception. The *New York Times* countered his statement that the newspaper had played down a story about an imminent American-sponsored invasion of Cuba by giving prominent play to Schlesinger's admission that, as a Kennedy aide, he had leaked a false cover story during one of the Cuban flaps. Schlesinger's complaint that Kennedy was ill-served by the papers which acquiesced in Kennedy's pleas to play down news hardly increases skeptics' confidence in any of the parties involved. Schlesinger implies that if the newspapers had violated Kennedy's invoking of national security by defiantly featuring the true story they might have prevented the President from following through on his own foolish plans. Schlesinger also admits to having felt uneasy when Kennedy induced the *New Republic* not to print, in Schlesinger's words, Karl Meyer's "careful, accurate and devastating account of CIA activities among Cuban refugees in Miami."

Such sober writers as Arthur Krock and Hanson Baldwin frequently scolded the Kennedy Administration for "news management." Even Kennedy, according to Sorensen, believed that his aide, Arthur Sylvester, had used unwise and unclear language when, after the Cuban missile crisis, the Assistant Secretary of Defense for Public Affairs stated bluntly that news was one of the "weapons with which we fight the Cold War" and the country had "the right, if necessary, to lie to save itself" from nuclear attack. Sylvester declined Kennedy's request that he admit his words "should have been more carefully phrased," and news management continued to exist in the Administration. Consequently, many skeptics decided thereafter to keep Sylvester's statement in mind when reading *any* government statement which could conceivably involve national security.

It would be dangerously naive for students of political affairs not to know that long before Machiavelli, and since, leaders of all forms of government have recognized that the control and generation of information was one of the most crucial elements of power. That political leaders should attempt to promote information favorable to their exercise of power and discourage other kinds of information is a normal part of the governing process not in itself unusual or reprehensible. The invocation of the term national security as a tool for expanding government control of information, however, increases to an alarming degree during crises, even in democracies. Also, the institutionalization of government generation and control of information has made it increasingly difficult for citizens to arrive at conclusions contrary to those the government wishes them to have.

The modern coordination and control of government information owes much to newsman and press secretary James Haggerty who worked first with Governor Dewey of New York and later with President Eisenhower. But most serious observers noticed that Kennedy and his aides dealing with information policy did more than any previous administration to control, coordinate, and centralize the flow of information to the public. This was of course carried very much further by Kennedy's successor who added a highly subjective and often eccentric personal element to information control which distinguishes it from what might have been otherwise assessed as merely a normal progression from Kennedy's practices.

No fair observer could deny that the country gained an important sense of responsibility from the ability of the Kennedy Administration to speak more with one voice in the areas of foreign and military affairs. But there were skeptics then and now who believed that Kennedy's controls prevented the country from getting all the information it should and ought legitimately to have for the evaluation of government policy and personnel. Some of the nation's most serious and respected writers and editors, as has been indicated, leveled specific complaints or charges at the Kennedy Administration in this respect. Any serious student of the Kennedy literature would do well to examine some of these before deciding what is to be believed. A general, fair-minded discussion of the problem is found in Harry Howe Ransom's *Can Democracy Survive the Cold War?* (New York: Doubleday Anchor Books, 1963, 623 pp.). For critical treatments, see William McGaffin and Erwin Knoll, *Anything But the Truth: The Credibility Gap—How the News is Managed in Washington* (New York: Putnam), 1968, and for earlier pieces see Lester Markel, "Management of the News," the *Saturday Review,* February 9, 1963, pp. 50–51; Hanson Baldwin, "Managed News—Our Peacetime Censorship," *The Atlantic Monthly,* 1963, pp. 53–59; Arthur Krock, "Mr. Kennedy's Management of the News," *Fortune,* March, 1963, pp. 82 ff., and Richard Rovere, "Letter from Washington," *New Yorker,* March 30, 1962, pp. 164–69.

Evaluations of news control in the Kennedy Administration as well as other recent administrations can be found in the annual reports of the Freedom of Information Committee of the Sigma Delta Chi national professional journalism fraternity and the reports of the Freedom of Information Center of the University of Missouri School of Journalism. Among the journalists who have done especially useful and creditable work in this area are Clark R. Mollenhoff, Louis M. Lyons, Erwin Knoll, J. V. Newton, Jr., and J. R. Wiggins. Their articles and columns help the critical reader make at least a rough estimate of how much of the necessary facts the reader of the Kennedy literature has.

To partially remedy this defect it is useful for the reader to be constantly aware that President Kennedy, just as any recent president, had as his central task the governing of a country during a perilous period in international affairs. Although he was more committed to the political education of the electorate than were most Presidents, neither he nor his aides could ever be expected to have as their main task the presentation of objective information to the public. In introducing *To Turn the Tide,* a volume of his presidential speeches, President Kennedy earnestly asks the reader to understand the inhibitions under which a president speaks and writes publicly. All his words are bound to be heard and acted upon by "adversaries, allies, neutrals, the Congress, and other members of the Administration as well as the diverse individuals and interest groups which compose the American electorate." Each, he wrote, must be taken into account.

In keeping with this invitation to critical awareness the reader should notice, for instance, that although some of the letters exchanged between Kennedy and Krushchev during the Cuban missile crisis have been made public, others have not, although at some future date a scholar or even the general public presumably will have access to them all.

As for an alleged connection between the withdrawal of Soviet nuclear missiles from Cuba and the United States withdrawal of nuclear missiles from Turkey and Italy some months later, the skeptical can only read the official American denial of a connection as well as reports from Turkey of a widespread belief there that a "deal" had been arranged between the United States and the Soviet Union. The interesting temporal relationship between the two withdrawals will spur the persistant researcher to look for further clues which might become available, but at this stage he will have to admit that there is not enough documentary evidence for making a solid judgment on this challenged report of the Kennedy Administration. The most skeptical researcher will even wish to ask how do we know that the Soviets did indeed remove their missiles from Cuba, there being no inspection to verify the fact, and he will discover that even this supposedly settled fact has been subjected to challenge.

In Kennedy's political life, only slightly less than in the elusive area of national security, it is likewise necessary to keep a critical eye open for conflicting versions of events as well as questions about which more information will have to be forthcoming or may never be known for the purpose of satisfactory assessment. For example, Kennedy intimates Theodore Sorensen, Evelyn Lincoln, Phillip Graham, and Pierre Salinger each have partially differing interpretations of what occurred and what the intentions of the principals were regarding Kennedy's offer of the vice-presidential nomination to Senator Johnson. Did Kennedy expect Johnson to accept and did the younger Senator intend the offer seriously? The careful researchers of this topic would note that an important version of this event has not yet been published. As the *New York Times* reported on July 19, 1966, "Senator Robert Kennedy has since said he has written his version of the incident for the Kennedy Library but that it will not be released soon." As the researcher searches further he will doubt that even the future availability of the Robert Kennedy version will mark the end of the trial of this story, because John F. Kennedy's press secretary Pierre Salinger has recorded his boss's reply to Salinger's inquiry about Kennedy's intentions in offering the Vice-Presidential nomination to Johnson. According to Salinger, Kennedy replied cryptically, "The whole story will never be known. And it is just as well that it won't." Thus the serious scholar is presented with a much more difficult task of verification than might be recognized by the casual reader.

There is a group of skeptics in Boston and scattered throughout the intellectual and reportorial community at large who have had some first-hand experience with the organizational enthusiasm of the Kennedy family and who are highly sensitive to the difficulty of determining exactly when any member of that family, John Fitzgerald included, did, said, or wrote anything on his own—regardless of how attributed—and when the substance was the product of numerous helping hands and minds. These skeptics think the Edwin O'Connor novel *All in the Family* (Little Brown, 1966), while fictionally exaggerated, has relevance to the career of John F. Kennedy. In this novel, the author of *The Last Hurrah* depicts a wealthy Boston Irish family which by the relentless employment of money, energy, and chicanery launches a mediocre son on a political career. Such skeptics link John F. Kennedy not only with the faults and naked amibition of his father but with the personal failings of his brothers as well. Sometimes this descended to a level of meanness. Youngest brother Edward, it would be recalled, had been punished at Harvard for having a classmate take an exam for him. Younger brother Robert had enveigled the family chauffeur in Riverdale to drive him in a Rolls Royce around his magazine route—later he had the chauffeur carry out the delivery chore alone. So with John, this line of association runs, you never could tell when money or charm or power had attracted talent to "stand in" for him or indeed to create him as he appeared in his public image.

Stripped of a petty, if natural, motivation of lesser men to chip a legendary figure down to size, this concern about the genuineness of the Kennedy literature has enough remaining legitimacy to merit careful consideration in such a bibliography as this. Therefore, an attempt is made further on in this essay to distinguish Kennedy's staffed or cooperative writing from that which is more demonstrably his, and in the titles selected for treatment in the bibliographical listing, attention has been given to probing, objective, and highly critical writing about John F. Kennedy in order to light a path toward an intellectually fair and realistic judgment.

Beside the problems of reconciling conflicting versions of events and resisting invitations to make judgments based upon partial information, the critical reader faces another problem of identifying news which is generated by an administration for its partisans and for the gullible, but which would not otherwise be considered as news at all. Far too many newsmen take the easy way out in passing on to their readers only slightly rewritten versions of government "handouts" as a substitute for careful cross-checking or for researching a story which an administration might not be so eager to bring to public attention. Joseph Kraft, one writer who does his homework, has cautioned us, "For the usual reasons of self esteem the news community clings to the conventional notion of a free and independent press arduously 'digging out' information . . . the myth is fostered by grave talk of the public's right to know. . . ." Kraft, who knows Washington practices as well as any writer has seen too much passing on of government handouts to believe the supposed conventional critical standards.

This bibliography attempts to help the serious reader in this respect by being critically selective in writers cited and by identifying those whose critical judgment is to be trusted, as well as identifying an occasional example of uncritical reporting of news generated by the Administration.

Moreover, the credibility of the literature of Kennedy's life presented fewer problems than the literature of his death. Hard-core skeptics believed Chief Justice Warren was speaking directly to them when, in February of 1964, he responded to a reporter's question about the release of Warren Commission testimony: "Yes, there will come a time. But it might not be in your lifetime. I am not referring to anything especially, but there may be some things that would involve security. This would be preserved but not made public." The Chief Justice's later statement that he had not meant this utterance seriously left lingering doubt for some.

Despite the prestige of the Commission Members and the quality of much of the Commission's testimony and evidence, it was buffeted by doubts from unexpected quarters having both sentimental and expert appeal. For example, Cardinal Cushing, who had been especially close to John F. Kennedy, told a press conference in the spring of 1967 he never believed the assassination of President Kennedy "was the work of one man." (See "Cushing—I Never Believed 1 Man Assassination Theory," *New York Post,* March 16, 1967). Some months later a world authority in forensic medicine and the investigation of bullet wounds, New York City's Chief Medical Examiner, Dr. Milton Halpern, issued a searching criticism of the autopsy evidence accepted by the Warren Commission, weaknesses of which contributed to the "aura of doubt and suspicion" that has enveloped its work. (See: "Halpern Criticizes Autopsy on JFK," *New York Post,* October 9, 1967. Critics of the critics of the Warren Report made a strong case that "None of the Report's critics have been able to suggest any other explanation that fits the known facts better than the Warren Commission's" and no alternative explanation of events as espoused by Commission critics received widespread acceptance. Nevertheless—and this the defenders of the Warren Commission found it difficult to understand—it was quite possible for readers to find unacceptable *both* the Commission Report and the alternative explanations which have been thus far offered. In fact, in 1968 Gallup and Harris polls showed that six out of every ten Americans think the Warren Commission did not tell the whole story in concluding that Oswald acted alone in assassinating the President.

Yet, despite blemishes just discussed, the bulk of the Kennedy literature remains believable. There is simply too much information amassed which can be cross-checked to expose internal inconsistencies for it to be otherwise. It must also be remembered that few political figures other than Kennedy would throw open their personal and political records to such a penetrating and incorruptible biographer as James MacGregor Burns. Furthermore, such astute journalists as Joseph Kraft, William Shannon, Murray Kempton, and Cabell Phillips are not easy to fool. Even the factual information and relative completeness of detail by admitted Kennedy partisans Sorensen and Schlesinger have held up solidly against attempts to disprove them, and it was Sorensen and Schlesinger themselves who voluntarily informed us of Kennedy news manipulation in order to give a more complete picture of the young President's Administration.

The interpretation of facts, of course, is up to each reader: for this, the skeptic's approach remains the best because it uses evidence, not testimonials, in evaluating significance.

Kennedy himself tended to be skeptical about the reliability of evidence. He complained, when preparing *Profiles in Courage,* that few trustworthy biographies had been written about American political figures. Presidents, he elaborated later, were given special credit for actions for which there were no alternatives: to know when the man made a *difference* was a difficult thing. As he told Schlesinger, "Who the hell can tell? Only the President himself can know what his real pressures and his real alternatives are. If you don't know that, how can you judge performance?" In the same skeptical mood, Kennedy had earlier declined an invitation from Arthur Schlesinger, Sr., to participate in a poll of historians and political scientists evaluating the Presidents, saying he would have done so gladly a year before becoming President but that now he was not so sure. (When the poll was published, Kennedy objected to the high rating of Woodrow Wilson, whom he considered a better writer than President, although he took some satisfaction in seeing Eisenhower ranked below Hoover. Eisenhower, who ranked 28th, was in Europe when the results were published, but Kennedy "decided some friends would send him a copy.")

LITERARY STYLE IN THE KENNEDY LITERATURE

Like much popular biography, journalism, and political writing, the Kennedy literature ranges from deplorable through indifferent to very good indeed. Kennedy's own books are generally quite readable: The prose is strong and clear even when treating complex subjects. Though the gravity of his subject and the steadily logical development of his mind made *Why England Slept* a minor best seller, it is the style of *Profiles in Courage* that was probably responsible for its enormous success. Readers appreciated the brevity of the chapters, the important point made with conciseness, the sprinkling of anecdotes throughout, and the insights into the outlandish behavior of Senators and their constituents.

Kennedy was proud of his writings. He kept the five books he had written, in special leather binding, on his desk at the White House office: *As We Remember Joe, Why England Slept, Profiles in Courage, The Strategy of Peace,* and *To Turn the Tide.* The last two volumes, containing his speeches, are judged by many to be more readable and enduring than Adlai Stevenson's similar efforts.

Unfortunately, the literature about Kennedy's personal life and of the workings of his mind is riddled with banal and one-dimensional treatments. (Mrs. Jacqueline Kennedy ran afoul of even poorer writing about her, and she will probably continue to do so.) The torrent of words on the Kennedy family brought forth this parody by Richard West in the *New Statesman* in May of 1966:

> Which Kennedy do you most enjoy reading about? Life-enhancing, life-affirming, wry, funny, coolly committed, amazingly young, tough-minded Jack? Caustic, cutting, thrusting, restless, aggressive, astonishingly mature, tough-minded, fun-loving, loyal, compulsively hard-working, ruthless Bobby? Or quiet, wry, life-affirming, life-enhancing, amazingly young, loyal, coolly ambitious, funny, surprisingly tough-minded Ted? There is much to be said for quiet, wry, astonishingly mature, seven-

year-old John. He has not yet been gushed about by drivelling Madison Avenue hacks and adoring professors."

West had adequate provocation for his outburst. He would not have been surprised either had he known that in November of 1962, the USIA distributed in comic book form a biography on Kennedy and that the President was featured in a "Superman" comic strip dealing with physical fitness.

However, the reader of the Kennedy literature can take solace from the fact that some of the least stylish writing by firsthand observers carries an excitement of its own because of the nature of the information revealed. For admirers of good prose, there is the exceptionally high quality to be found in the graceful phrases of Schlesinger, Joseph Kraft, William Shannon, Murray Kempton, Emmet Hughes, and Benjamin Bradlee.

KENNEDY AS A WRITER

To write of Kennedy as an author, journalist, critic, and consort of writers first, and as the subject of biographers last, may seem strange, but he was all of these before he became a subject worthy of biography. John F. Kennedy ultimately became one of the two dozen greatest selling authors, including writers of fiction or nonfiction, in American history. His *Profiles in Courage* sold well over four million copies in America in paperback form and had more than a score of foreign translations as well. His writings had a greater impact on his political career and the legend he left than their strictly literary merit would warrant, and they reveal only a little less about his ideas than the criticism of them by other authors. Of special interest to the serious student are the origins of Kennedy's political writings during his career as Senator and President; this controversial subject needs clarification before the quality of Kennedy's literary writings can be properly evaluated.

Kennedy's literary development paralleled his development as a statesman. However, when he reached the heights of his political career, he found that the pressures of time and an easy access to a crew of speech drafters conflicted with, and all but put an end to, his career as a literary writer. In his early career, leisure time permitted him to write pieces of popular history or thoughtful articles on public affairs which merited publication in such diverse journals as the *Reader's Digest,* *Harper's* Magazine, and the prestigious *Foreign Affairs.* Later, as a Senator and Presidential candidate, he could, at best, produce a kind of "staffed literature" as head of a team of writers.

Had Kennedy lived on, it was his intention to bring the two vocations—political and literary writing—together again. He planned, for a period at least, to give the writing of his Presidential memoirs all the concentration of his talent. His other plans upon leaving the White House included lecturing, perhaps running a newspaper, returning to Congress, and increasing his literary output considerably. But before he wrote, he would have travelled, because movement, vitality, and finding out facts firsthand were always more important to him than the act of writing what he had learned or observed.

Kennedy was being serious as well as humorous when he told a business group only four weeks after entering the White House: "Whether I serve one or two terms in the Presidency, I will find myself at the end of that period at what might be called the awkward age—too old to begin a new career and too young to write my memoirs."

The question of where Kennedy ranks in regard to other presidential writers deserves at least passing mention. Kennedy was, of course, by far the best selling writer of any man who occupied the White House. The spectacular success of the writing of Ulysses S. Grant, incidentally, stands as proof that it is not necessary for a public figure to be an intellectual in order to write for a wide audience. The most recent brilliant intellectual and writer to occupy the White House was Woodrow Wilson, whom Kennedy could not be said to match either in political analysis or, for that matter, even in managing Congress. Wilson wrote his impressive *Congressional Government* at the age of twenty-eight. This work has contributed to the thinking of tens of thousands and enjoys both respect and considerable circulation even today. In brilliance of political analysis Kennedy was, of course, not in a league with extraordinary presidential writers Jefferson and Madison. But then these comparisons—interesting mainly because they reveal that good writing has never been an automatic bar to the White House—are unfair in that Kennedy never tried to be nor thought of himself as a profound social thinker, but as a popularizer of history and a special kind of modern educator-at-large. In a league closer to his own he can be compared most favorably as a writer when matched with Presidents Eisenhower and Truman.

HIS PREPARATION AS A WRITER

Kennedy had a good deal going for him as a potential writer. In the first place, the environment he was born into afforded an excellent subject for writing—politics. His paternal grandfather, Patrick J. Kennedy, was a Boston-bred Irishman who turned his saloon into a political caucus room and campaign headquarters. He was, in fact, part of a coalition of Democratic bosses which included Kennedy's maternal grandfather, John F. "Honey Fitz" Fitzgerald, a very successful political figure who became mayor of Boston. A clergyman remarked of "Honey Fitz" in 1906: "Our present mayor has the distinction of appointing more saloon keepers and bartenders to public office than any previous mayor." One of the earliest events Kennedy recalled was walking or riding a Locomobile around the wards of Boston with his grandfather as the politician performed the legendary "Irish Switch." This consisted of shaking one voter's hand, talking animatedly with another, and smiling into the eyes of the third. The stream of political lore and hard-headed canniness about the brass knuckles aspect of politics which flowed from the grandfathers' careers never left the Kennedy family even when they all deserted the saloons for higher duties.

Kennedy's father, Joseph Patrick Kennedy, decided on financial speculation and investments as a means of establishing himself and his family. Although Joseph Kennedy graduated from Harvard, John Kennery admitted, "I've almost never seen him read a serious book." However, Joseph Kennedy wrote one in 1936, entitled *I'm for Roosevelt,* published by Reynal and Hitchcock, and had earlier, in 1927, edited *The Story of the Films* for A. W. Shaw and Co. Joseph Kennedy carried on the family interest in politics, contributing to national campaigns and serving Franklin Roosevelt in high federal regulatory commissions and as Ambassador to the Court of St. James.

The plain fact was that politics was in all the Kennedy's Irish blood. With the coming of a new generation and a rise in social status (and after majoring in government at Harvard), John Kennedy would explain his interest in politics in literary terms. He enjoyed quoting one of his favorite authors, John Buchan (Lord Tweedmuir): "Public life is the crown of a career and to the young man, it is the worthiest ambition. Politics is the greatest and most honorable profession." (As he himself prepared to carry on the family's political fortunes, Robert Kennedy wrote this quote into the 1963 edition of his late brother's *Profiles in Courage*.)

Unfortunately, John Kennedy was too removed from the Boston wards to write the racy descriptions of them which novelist Edwin O'Connor could (although Kennedy could enjoy Boston politics privately while stating publicly that this was not the way things ought to be done). Instead, Senator Kennedy contributed to the *New York Times Book Review* in September, 1959, a high-minded review of Professor Joseph Hutchmacher's book on Boston politics.

Kennedy's zeal for politics and for writing about politics was also spurred on by the family's search for status. In his review of Hutchmacher's book mentioned above, Kennedy remarks that "the struggle for status and power by the new immigrants had a special flavor in Massachusetts." The snobbery and exclusion which the Irish met were fiercely resented, and subconsciously admired. Well aware of the symbols of the struggle, Kennedy reminds us, "Harvard, Beacon Hill and South Boston are almost continguous." Kennedy notes how "political life and action brought status and prestige and ultimately a sense of citizenship to huddled masses that made the long journey from Europe."

The social and economic snobbery of Boston and Harvard, described brilliantly in Cleveland Amory's *The Proper Bostonians,* was extraordinary. Snobbery drove Joseph Kennedy from Boston, and pursued his family in summer homes, where they were accepted in predominantly Catholic Nantasket, but blackballed from the country club at the "Old Boston family" beach of Cohasset. One of Joseph Kennedy's daughters complained to Sorensen years later that the old Massachusetts families summering around Hyannisport still refused to have anything to do with the Kennedys. A basic belief expressed by Joseph Kennedy was that "the measure of a man's life is not the money he's made. It's the kind of family he's raised. In that I've been mighty lucky." But having raised what he thought a good family and having made a fortune, he still found himself spoken of in Boston as "the Irishman." "What in Hell do you have to do to get to be an American around here?" he once stormed.

To become a millionaire or ambassador or President would naturally help, in the father's view, and, in a smaller way, so would writing. After Joseph Kennedy had written his *I'm For Roosevelt* at a strategic date in the 1936 campaign that was suggested by Roosevelt, he badgered the President until Roosevelt finally sent him a handwritten note, now framed at the Kennedy's Hyannisport home, testifying that it was "a grand book." The elder Kennedy had thought it wise to insert a line in the book declaring, "I have no political ambitions for myself or my children," but the results of the book certainly weren't bound to do any harm in that direction. And when John Kennedy succeeded in having his Harvard honors thesis published under the title *Why England Slept,* his father wrote him from his London Embassy post: "You would be surprised how a book that really makes the grade with high-class people stands you in good stead for years to come . . . I remember that in the report you are asked to make after 25 years to the Committee at Harvard, one of the questions is 'What books have you written?' and there is no doubt you have done yourself a great deal of good." According to biographer Burns the Ambassador sent copies of his son's *Why England Slept* to Professor Harold Laski, Winston Churchill and—lest anyone be overlooked—the Queen of England herself!

Despite his own book and ambassadorship, Joseph Kennedy was passed over for a place on the Harvard Board of Overseers, and he later got himself into the awkward position of publicly "declining" an honorary degree from that University which had not been formally offered. His son John Kennedy was also passed over in 1955 after being considered for the Harvard Board of Overseers, causing him what some believed to be one of the greatest disappointments of his life. However, in 1957, after he received the Pulitzer Prize for his *Profiles in Courage,* Kennedy was given his Overseers hat along with an honorary degree, proving his father's observation about "high-class people." As a result of *Profiles in Courage,* Kennedy was also chosen by the United States Senate to head a special committee to select the five most outstanding senators in the nation's history—a distinguished honor for a young senator not considered an "insider."

Besides having a spur as well as encouragement to write, Kennedy early developed an important attribute for a writer: a point of view. Throughout his life he read biographies of men of affairs as well as books of history, and he was one of the few fourteen-year-olds at Choate to subscribe to and read the *New York Times* daily. As a writer he studied those crucial points in history when men of decision and social forces interact. The not-quite-answerable question of which factor is more responsible, the man or the event, intrigued Kennedy, and he made an attempt to solve the problem in his two most serious books. *Why England Slept* emphasized social forces, showing how these forces made rearmament almost impossible, though men of decision shared a portion of the blame. In *Why England Slept,* Kennedy complained that Americans are always interested in personalities, but very little in facts. Later, in his *Profiles in Courage,* he sought out situations where the burden of decision was clearly on the actor and the actor knew it.

In addition to the recurring theme of men versus social forces, Kennedy absorbed from the European atmosphere of Munich and rearmament almost an obsession with the role of military might in foreign policy. The military aspects of foreign policy which set the tone of his first book remained a predominant theme in his writings and speeches during his later Senate years and Presidency. Closely associated with it was the concept, to which intellectuals are particularly addicted, of two systems in deadly conflict, where only the stronger will survive.

Travel was also important to the education of Kennedy as a writer; it gave him, at an early age, the necessary confidence to make authoritative statements, as evidenced in his *Why England Slept,* written when he was twenty-three. Later, the notes on a trip to Europe and Asia in 1951 provided material for reports to Congress, public speeches, and articles on foreign policy. But his travels in his college years had the most lasting effect; although Kennedy was only one generation removed from the Boston Irish, his exposure to Britain in many ways left him with a remarkably British outlook. Murray Kempton notes that it is the British model of Kennedy which predominates in most journalistic reminiscences about the President.

In Britain, Kennedy was able to see firsthand the difficulties of a peace-loving democracy confronting an expansive, authoritarian system (in this case, fascism). It is this confrontation theme which haunts most of his major foreign policy statements, although whether or not the analogy applied to later decades and places where democracy confronted communism is highly questionable.

He also came to admire the cool and unemotional British intellectual attitude toward foreign affairs. All his life Kennedy continued to read British journals with unusual respect, and he was greatly concerned with how his writings and statements would be received in intelligent British circles. That his *Why England Slept* was as much of a best seller in England as at home was a source of enormous pleasure to him. A standard of excellence to Kennedy was that his writing and speeches make sense to and be appreciated by his British friend Sir David Ormsby-Gore (Lord Harlech). Because of his concern with the judgment of fair-minded, intelligent British observers, the Boston-Irish Kennedy avoided parochial statements on foreign affairs commonly made by other American politicians. During Kennedy's Presidency, the French were certainly justified in complaining about the close relationship between "les Anglo-Saxons."

Young Kennedy's travels permitted him to compare what he saw in Europe with books he had read by seasoned observers, particularly John Gunther. His observations during his European tours in the summer of 1937 and the spring semester of 1939 were unmarked by preconceptions as he talked with people in Western and Eastern Europe, including Russia. From Russia, Kennedy journeyed to Palestine and in a letter to his father, then U.S. ambassador in London, he loyally attempted to sort the tangled strands of British-Arab-Jewish grievances.

Of the various observations Kennedy made in his travels, his letter to his father from Spain in the summer of 1937, quoted by Burns, is most interesting. The Harvard government major believed that the British had a strategic interest in Spain. But, "although most people in the U.S. are for Franco, and while I felt that perhaps it would be far better for Spain if Franco should win—as he would strengthen and unite Spain—yet at the beginning the [Loyalist] government was right morally speaking, as its program was similar to the New Deal. . . . Their attitude towards the Church was just a reaction to the strength of the Jesuits who had become too powerful—the affiliation between Church and State much too close."

The budding author's observations on Spain would have outraged partisans on either side of that tragic battlefield, but no one could accuse him of having accepted the current clichés of the antagonists.

Kennedy's eclectic taste helped him avoid becoming a stereotyped bore—the problem of the average political writer. His father, a man of far stronger, sometimes violent opinions likewise avoided stereotyping and urged the attribute on his sons. Senator John Kennedy exclaimed of his father in 1953, "Do you realize that his first choice for the Presidency last year was Senator Taft and his second Justice Douglas!" Kennedy's later choice of aides as well as his admiration for Republican Senator Saltonstall and Governor Nelson Rockefeller also showed the same shying away from a consistent line as was exhibited in his choice of subjects for *Profiles in Courage*.

THE CIRCUMSTANCES OF KENNEDY'S WRITING

Of course, this emphasis on the more practical aspects of how a person is motivated and learns to write is somewhat misleading. One should not overlook the fact that Kennedy learned to read and write at Riverdale, Canterbury, Choate, and Harvard. He was a gentleman "C" scholar on balance except for his major field of government and in history. He read widely about nationalism, fascism and colonialism, and took a minor post on the *Harvard Crimson*. But his significant move, after a semester in Europe in 1939, was to write an honors thesis entitled "Appeasement at Munich." In developing and documenting his thesis, Kennedy studied *Parliamentary Debates,* Foreign Office Statements, *The Times* of London, and other journals. Ambassador Joseph Kennedy sent him a great deal of advice about the possibility of publishing the thesis. Burns, who is not a biographer to allow any fault to pass his notice, even notes that a few phrases "taken almost verbatim from a letter from his father" were added when the thesis became a book. But all are in agreement that this book is the work of John Kennedy and not a staff product. Joseph Kennedy's friend, Arthur Krock of the *New York Times,* suggested an agent for his son's manuscript and also gave the book its title. The title *Why England Slept* seemed to imply that Kennedy's analysis would delve deeper into the reasons for the conditions described in Winston Churchill's collection of speeches, *While England Slept*.

Harper and Brothers, later to be Kennedy's major publisher, turned the manuscript down, but Wilfred Funk snapped it up and sold 40,000 copies here and as many in Britain—probably making John Kennedy a more popular American in Britain than his father, the U.S. ambassador. Another Joseph Kennedy friend, Henry Luce, had insisted in his introduction to the book that it ought to sell a million copies!

The most important writing Kennedy did during the war, he wrote on coconut. With a knife he carved "Eleven Alive Native Knows Posit and Reefs Nauru Island Kennedy," and gave the coconut to a native who, although he understood no English, delivered it and thereby brought help to the stranded members of Kennedy's crashed PT boat in the South Pacific. Sent back to Boston with lingering effects of malaria and a back injury caused by the sinking of his PT boat, he planned, while in a hospital, a book of tributes to his brother Joe who had been killed in a plane crash flying an almost impossible bombing mission in Europe. Five hundred copies of a privately printed, slim maroon volume soon appeared, edited by John Kennedy and entitled *As We Remember Joe*.

Toward the end of the war Kennedy put in a brief stint as a journalist and the editors of *Editor and Publisher* (November 30, 1963, p. 65) are partially correct in saying that Kennedy always kept a reporter's outlook. He wrote for the International News Service owned by William Randolph Hearst, for whom Joseph Kennedy had once worked as a consultant at $10,000 a week.

Writing from the "G.I.'s viewpoint," Kennedy in his first columns covered the San Francisco Conference which formed the United Nations organization; these columns may be found in the New York *Journal American* (April 28, 30, and May 2–5, 7, 8, 14, 16, 18, 19, 21, 23 and 28, 1945), as well as in Hearst newspapers of other American cities. Not one of them is of enough importance to merit annotation under the Kennedy writings, but one notes the development of his view from sympathetic optimism to a realization that the nations gathered in San Francisco were unwilling to give up any meaningful sovereignty and that only a skeletal organization with very limited powers would result. He wrote of Russian recalcitrance and of the talk heard in the corridors of an impending war between the Soviets and their former allies. He did, however, approve of the new organization, although he admitted that it represented most of the same compromises which paralyzed the League of Nations, and he hoped for future cooperation between America, Russia, and England. A group of unexceptional articles from London on the British election of 1945 (to be found also in the New York *Journal American,* June 24, July 10 and 27, 1945) closed his career as a newspaperman.

There is evidence that reporter John Kennedy in London just missed publishing a "scoop" which would have made these dispatches memorable and his news career quite promising. Certainly he had enough knowledge and empathy with the British to give him courage of judgment, but he chose to listen to a political muse which shies from originality instead of his writers muse which says "tell it like it is." In a reminiscent mood, Senator Kennedy recalled to reporter Peter Lisagor his 1945 experience thus:

> One of my first stories predicted that Winston Churchill and the Tory Party were going to lose the election to Attlee and Labor. No sooner did that story hit New York than I got a rocket from Hearst, practically charging me with being out of my mind. Well, in the next several days, I gradually worked it around to where Churchill had rallied and now looked like an easy winner. If I had stuck to my original story, I'd have been a red-hot prophet.

WHO WROTE PROFILES IN COURAGE?

Kennedy wrote *Profiles in Courage.* However, he was sufficiently far along the path to "staff literature" by 1955 that his authorship was brought seriously into question, first by word of mouth and finally by Drew Pearson on a television show. The charge so lingered on that, even after his election when, as President-elect, Kennedy was interviewing Robert McNamara for a cabinet position, the future Secretary of Defense asked Kennedy bluntly if he had really written the book which McNamara much admired.

It is perhaps as well to establish for the reader of this bibliography exactly how the book was written, and in doing so, to clarify why *Profiles in Courage* and *Why England Slept* are treated here as Kennedy's own literature, which such subsequent works as *The Strategy of Peace, To Turn the Tide,* and *The Burden and the Glory* are treated as "staff literature," that is, a cooperative literature produced by both a staff and an extraordinarily busy Kennedy.

Like *As We Remember Joe,* the idea for *Profiles in Courage* originated while Kennedy was in a hospital bed, but long before that he had been intrigued with political figures who had withstood the pressures of their constituencies to take a daring political stand which they believed to be correct. As a result of an article with the suggested title of "Patterns of Political Courage" which Kennedy submitted to *Harper's* Magazine, the Harper publishing house suggested a book of similar pieces, and Evan Thomas, who later urged the title *Profiles in Courage,* became Kennedy's able editor.

In his preface to *Profiles in Courage,* Kennedy is quite generous, specific, and unpretentious in his appreciations for help on what was to be his most famous book. His chief thanks justifiably go to his aide Theodore C. Sorensen for "assistance in the assembly and preparation of the material upon which this book is based." He also shows appreciation to James MacGregor Burns, Arthur Krock (who suggested Taft's courageous criticisms of the Nuremberg Trials) and aides of the Library of Congress for "important contributions to the selection of examples" in the book. Professor Jules Davids of Georgetown University, Washington, D.C., Kennedy states, "assisted materially in the preparation of several chapters." For editorial criticisms of various kinds he thanks Professors Allan Nevins, Arthur Holcombe, Walter Johnson, and Arthur Schlesinger. This is hardly the preface of someone intending to deceive his readers; neither, of course, is it evidence of the solitary scholar working away in the library until closing time.

Most of the book was written on a board propped up before him as he lay on his back convalescing at his father's home in Palm Beach, Florida. Other parts of it were dictated to a secretary; the introduction and concluding chapters were completed after his return to the Senate. *Profiles in Courage,* begun in January, 1955, was finally published January 1, 1956.

Edward Weeks, in a book review for the *Atlantic Monthly* immediately attested to the book's authenticity. One of the best things about it, he wrote, "is that it is handmade. I mean written without the assistance of a public relations office." The book's hard-headed idealism also appealed to the *New York Times* reviewer Cabell Phillips, who told his New Year's readers that a "first-rate politician has written a thoughtful and persuasive book about political integrity." (A related Kennedy article, "The Challenge of Political Courage," had appeared in the *New York Times Magazine,* December 19, 1955.) Kennedy sent off autographed copies of the book to an enormous number of friends and colleagues, and he and Sorensen wrote other *Profile*-type articles for *Harper's,* the *Readers' Digest,* and other periodicals.

The book remained near the top of the national best seller list longer than any other nonfiction book of 1956. On its undeniable merit, and with some help from Kennedy's friend Arthur Krock, who was on the Pulitzer Prize awards committee, the book won that committee's prize. The five-hundred-dollar stipend Kennedy collected was donated to the United Negro College Fund. *Profiles* also won a Notable Book Award of the American Library Association. It was later translated into more than a score of foreign languages.

POLITICAL CONSEQUENCES OF *PROFILES*

Kennedy's office staff believed that the favorable attention attracted by *Profiles in Courage* was largely responsible for the Senator's sharp rise in popularity polls and helped win for him more prominent consideration for the Vice Presidential nomination in 1956 and the Presidential nomination in 1960. Fletcher Knebel's piece on Kennedy in Eric Sevareid's *Candidates, 1960* had the lofty title, "The Pulitzer Prize Entry."

"Would that my enemy should write a book," is a legendary curse offered by the scholar-critic. Obviously Kennedy's writing could, and did, hardly have anything but a positive effect on his political fortunes. However, he was not quite immune from this curse; Edwin Canham, editor of the *Christian Science Monitor,* wrote in a review of the book, Kennedy "must watch his step in the future, for he has set up high standards of political integrity for comparison."

After the book was published, one highly placed Democrat remarked that we needed someone who could live courage, not only write about it. By the time this statement reached the cocktail party circles it was transformed into "we need less profile and more courage." The book, after all, had been written during a period when the question of contemporary courage and cowardice centered around McCarthyism. This controversy didn't find its way into *Profiles,* although the book said of courage, "Some admire its virtue in other men and other times, but fail to comprehend its current potentialities." "It is an opportunity," Kennedy added, "which sooner or later is presented to all of us." His critics asked, when will Kennedy's time come? Those who overlooked Kennedy's heroism in the South Pacific (and were, at a later date, ready to concede his gritty courage during the Cuban missile crisis) kept harboring reservations during Kennedy's late Senate years whether the author of *Profiles in Courage* would ever be deserving of a chapter in his own book.

It was on Pearl Harbor Day, December 7, 1957, when Drew Pearson, as mentioned earlier, charged on an ABC-TV program that Kennedy was not the true author of *Profiles*. The result: Kennedy and his secretary, Mrs. Evelyn Lincoln, rushed to his Senate office and together they searched out the yellow pads and notebooks in his handwriting as well as other material; these he soon made available to callers as proof of the book's true authorship. His aides had never seen him so upset.

The Senator, by now an unannounced Presidential candidate, seemed to believe that his career could be seriously affected if this charge was not refuted, but he was mainly angered, as Sorensen quoted him later, because the charge "challenges my ability to write the book, my honesty in signing it, and my integrity in accepting the Pulitzer Prize."

In the most amusing part of his book, *Kennedy,* Sorensen tells how, just prior to the ABC network's retraction of the charge, an ABC vice president questioned Senator Kennedy as to whether the rumor was true that Sorensen had personally boasted of writing *Profiles*. Perhaps, he coaxed Kennedy, Sorensen had said it when drinking or when mad at Kennedy. The Senator snapped back that Sorensen didn't drink and had never become mad at him. Interestingly, Sorensen admits that he *did* "ghost write" ABC's retraction statement!

KENNEDY'S STAFF LITERATURE

Kennedy was vain enough to deter photographers from publishing photos of him wearing reading glasses, but he was certainly not so vain that he wished to have it thought that during the busiest time of his political career he did all his own writing of speeches and statements. At the present time, the system of Presidential staff preparation of official literature and political speeches is so sufficiently established that little needs to be said about it here other than to indicate in what way Kennedy's use of staff literature differed from other Presidents' since its institutionalization under Franklin D. Roosevelt.

Most of the public came to accept Roosevelt's famous speeches and phrases as his own and, in retrospect, paid little attention to whether they were his own spontaneous replies at a press conference or, instead, a political thrust carefully honed by Robert Sherwood or others. Truman and Eisenhower audiences often as not were relieved at having a speech writer make their listeners' task easier. Not only did the idea of there being something essentially "phony" about staff preparation of speeches almost disappear, but even the slightly pejorative term "ghost writer" came to be used less and less in describing these staffers. Almost every political scholar knows that the tremendous number of messages a President sends to Congress, together with the many Executive orders which require only his signature, cannot possibly be his handiwork alone. He also knows that a President running for re-election, and who has to deliver eight different speeches a day in the heat of the campaign, obviously doesn't write them all himself. The basic question is whether or not the President is aware of what is in the material prepared by aides intimately acquainted with his thinking, and whether or not what is signed or uttered by the President seems consistent with what is known of the signator or speaker.

The chief factor which distinguished Kennedy's staff literature from that of other modern Presidents who have made such use of it was his degree of dependence upon one aide, Sorensen. Some Presidents had delivered speeches written by one writer to which they contributed little or nothing at all. More often, Presidents brought together the work of a number of writers, the President himself adding the finishing touches. But never before Kennedy had a President so completely merged his thinking and phrasing with one person so that in speechwriting they were one. Kennedy's collected speeches made in his last Senate years and in the Presidency form the major part of his writings; one should not have undue faith in the ability of computer machines to unscramble what was Kennedy's and what was Sorensen's in a given speech.

Alan Otten, writing in *The Kennedy Circle,* gives a striking picture of how this teamwork struck reporters. Once, when Kennedy lost his voice during the 1960 campaign, Sorensen, glancing at papers in his hand, apparently read a Kennedy campaign speech, including Kennedy-style jokes and some of Kennedy's favorite quotations. "Actually," Otten writes, "reporters learned later the papers were blank. The speech came from a mind so saturated with Kennedy thoughts and approach that it could speak perfect Kennedy."

It is true that aides other than Sorensen helped on some speeches. Schlesinger, Myer Feldman, and Richard Goodwin wrote or collaborated on speeches; advice came from other aides, appropriate to the subject matter; and scores of politicians, professors, and writers outside the Executive branch sent in ideas, phrases, and briefings. But no one quite fitted Kennedy's style the way Sorensen did. Schlesinger, for instance, acknowledges that Kennedy found his speech drafts too Stevensonian, the words too fancy, and the sentences too complicated. All the other speech drafters admit that Sorensen was the President's principal writing collaborator.

It took Sorensen several years before he became an alter ego to Kennedy. Kennedy's speeches were written for how they would sound, not how they would read, a point their readers should keep in mind. After Sorensen made a trip to California with Kennedy in a 1956 campaign swing to study at firsthand the Senator's speaking style and gestures, their resemblances became almost unnerving to some observers. The degree to which Sorensen subordinated his personality and ego to those of Kennedy was remarked upon so often that Kennedy used to ask reporters to "lay off Ted," remarking, "They're always riding him about that." Sorensen admits: "Some say that in time I talked and gestured as well as thought and wrote like the Senator. I doubt that he ever thought so, but occasionally for reasons of time more than mischief, he would have me assume his identity on the telephone." Sorensen says accurately that their extremely close professional relationship "forged a bond of intimacy in which there were few secrets and no illusions."

In his excellent descriptions of general speech preparations and the drafting of specific speeches such as Kennedy's Inaugural Address and his American University Address, Sorensen makes it clear that Kennedy set the subject and general ideas for his speeches, and edited them, added or deleted sections. Both Sorensen and Schlesinger offer interesting examples of the substantial changes Kennedy made in their speech drafts.

However, it was Kennedy's style the writers adapted to, not the other way around—the short words, short sentences, and alliteration, the humor and the favorite quotations were Kennedy's and Sorensen had to learn them Kennedy's way. But once it is established that the President was in full charge of the words he uttered, Sorensen's contribution must not be underestimated. Evelyn Lincoln, who knew as much about this contribution as anyone else, wrote that "The creation of a Kennedy speech was always a joint effort, with Ted and the President drawing on each other's ideas, but many of the most effective and memorable phrases were Ted's contributions."

To this must be added Burns' statements that the creation of a Kennedy speech was often a hectic effort, also. For example, a whole flurry of articles went out from Kennedy's Senate office, articles over which he and Sorensen struggled and which were sometimes researched by others on the staff. Most writers on Kennedy quote Burns' laudatory phrase that Kennedy was the largest Congressional user of the services of the Library of Congress, and some recall that his office produced as much as a dozen major articles and speeches a month. But they fail to quote Burns' illuminating previous paragraph which indicated the kind of atmosphere in which much of this information was turned into speeches and articles, an atmosphere which must have affected the Kennedy contributions to it. "At times the office looked like a five ring circus," Burns observed, "as Kennedy simultaneously performed as a senator, committee member, Massachusetts politician, author, and Presidential candidate."

Kennedy gave his most serious personal attention to foreign policy pieces and those dealing with labor, subjects which reflected his two major Senate committee assignments. Some articles appear to have been written primarily to get the Kennedy name publicized, such as one entitled "What My Illness Taught Me," for the *American Weekly*, and another on brotherhood for *Parade*. But many of them, while serving a similar purpose, did represent real Kennedy interest and helped fulfill his role as public educator. Most of them are either not of sufficient interest to merit annotation in this book or are represented in the collections cited in the annotations.

The very mildly reformist image Kennedy wished to project was represented in articles "To Keep the Lobbyist Within Bounds," *New*

York Times Magazine, February 19, 1956, p. 11 f., and "Take the Academies Out of Politics," *Saturday Evening Post,* June 2, 1956, pp. 36–37 ff. In the latter, Kennedy told how he established his own merit system for recommending applicants to the military academies.

His concern with reviving the depressed economy of New England and his desire to become identified as the leader in this effort were reflected in "What's the Matter with New England," *New York Times Magazine,* November 8, 1953. Work on the New England economy was one of the first assignments Kennedy gave to Sorensen, a Nebraskan. The economic background for these articles was largely contributed by Professor Seymour Harris of Harvard.

Kennedy was quite knowledgeable about labor, especially union matters. On labor questions he had the able staff assistance of Ralph Dungan and later, when necessary, the Senator called on the expertise of Harvard Professor Archibald Cox. Articles on labor signed by Kennedy were "The Floor Beneath Wages Is Gone," *New Republic,* July 20, 1953, pp. 14–15, and "What's Wrong with Social Security," *American Magazine,* October, 1953, pp. 19 ff.

A surprising number of Kennedy speeches and articles on foreign policy dealt with Vietnam, an area about which he spoke with considerable definiteness after a brief visit there. "What Should the U.S. Do in Indochina?" *Foreign Policy Bulletin,* May 15, 1954, pp. 4 ff., was followed by "America's Stake in Vietnam," *Vital Speeches,* August 1, 1956, pp. 617–619. Kennedy warned America with a quotation from T. E. Lawrence: "War on rebellion is messy and slow, like cutting soup with a knife." However, Kennedy's solutions still left Vietnam pretty soupy. His concern, first expressed in *Why England Slept,* about the problem of dragging the anchor of public opinion in foreign policy is reiterated in "Foreign Policy is the People's Business," *New York Times Magazine,* August 8, 1954, pp. 5 ff.

These are examples of the kinds of staffed literature which Kennedy wrote during his Senate years. They will be mainly of interest to those researching Kennedy's relation to one of the topics covered or to those who wish to read everything which appeared under his name. On the whole, those speeches of his late Senate years which were collected in *The Strategy of Peace* are superior in thought.

KENNEDY'S STANDING IN THE WORLD OF LETTERS

Modest as it was in quantity and literary merit, Kennedy's writing coupled with his interest in good writing and his rapport with writers gave him a position in the world of letters which was important to his career and to the legend which lives after him. There was an interest in his writing and his literary judgments in serious quarters which could not conceivably have been the result of a family arrangement or of public relations. His first book, *Why England Slept,* for instance, was reviewed not only in the *Times* (London) *Literary Supplement* and the *Spectator,* but also in the *New Yorker,* the *New York Times, Current History, Commonweal, New Republic, Saturday Review of Literature,* and the *Wisconsin Library Bulletin,* among other journals. His next book, *Profiles in Courage,* won reviews in additional publications such as the *American Political Science Review, Atlantic Monthly, Foreign Affairs,* and *Nation.* Interestingly, his subsequent books of collected speeches, treated here as staff literature, while gaining creditable notice, received considerably less widespread serious critical attention despite the author's emergence into worldwide fame. However, three presses or publishers thought his Inaugural Address of sufficient literary merit and import to have it printed and distributed privately to friends.

Furthermore, after Kennedy's prize winning second book, when another writer published a book on subjects ranging from American history and politics to international and military affairs, there was a possibility Senator Kennedy might be called upon to review it by editors of such journals as *Saturday Review, New York Times Book Review,* and *Reporter*—to mention only interesting Kennedy reviews resulting from such requests. Sometimes Kennedy's literary attentions seemed particularly consequential, as when even practical-minded Washington politicians sensed some connection between Kennedy's review of General James Gavin's book *War and Peace in the Space Age* and his later sending the General to Paris as ambassador.

Kennedy's very brief stint as a Hearst reporter and widely known regular scanning of a remarkable number of newspapers and journals helped him to identify with journalists and editors. But he was also the delight of many librarians. He would find time to send a letter to one of their journals or a presidential message to their association meeting, and also, they would notice a slightly increased circulation of a neglected quality political biography or autobiography in conjunction with the printed or verbal report that Kennedy was reading or had appreciated such a volume. *The New York Times,* for example, carried a résumé of Senator Kennedy's current reading lists, July 21, 1958 edition. As Senator, he was known as the busiest congressional user of the Library of Congress and aspiring politicians and administrative aides were known to read certain contemporary books because they had been spotted on the shelves of Kennedy's Senate office and conversation proved he had read them. Later members of university communities combed the list of books placed in Kennedy's White House library to see if the title of one of their colleagues was so honored, and political scientists and American historians felt reassured when noting that books on the presidency which they assigned in classes were on the shelves of the cabinet room and Kennedy's Oval Office and at times were put to use.

Distinguished historians were genuinely interested in what President Kennedy would have to say in his speech at the ceremony marking the publication of the long awaited Adams Papers. The President's aide and sometimes speech writer Arthur Schlesinger prepared the first draft, but Kennedy took the speech over and made it his own, as a President and a popular historian having ideas of his own about this earlier President from Massachussetts.

Kennedy certainly cultivated writers and intellectuals in general in numerous ways. His speech delivered to alumni at Harvard University on June 14, 1956, later printed under the title "The Intellectual and the Politician," called for the kind of alliance he later largely achieved. Some months earlier he had cast a similar appeal to women in a piece entitled "Brothers I presume?" carried in *Vogue,* April 1, 1956, which deplored and proposed remedies for "the current hostility between the political and literary worlds." At various points in his presidency, particularly after the Bay of Pigs fiasco and toward his last months in the White House, intellectuals wrote stinging criticism of the President, but often with the expectation that he had the capacity to benefit from it. Literary critic and social historian Alfred Kazin, after lunching with the President, soon threw him a small rock of criticism but wrapped it in a bouquet—the flattering title of his critique reading "The President and Other Intellectuals" (*American Scholar* [Autumn, 1961], pp. 498–516).

No one could fail to notice that Kennedy had a way with fiction writers and poets as well. He was known to read only a very modest amount of fiction (and that included James Bond novels) but Norman Mailer was pleasantly surprised at the Democratic Convention in 1960 when the then "total politician" Kennedy spoke to him about *Deer Park,* one of Mailer's lesser known and least successful novels. This seemed innocently delightful until it became known that Kennedy also had spoken to author James Michener about *Fires of Spring* and to Eugene Burdick about *The Ninth Wave.*

Much of the country and particularly intellectuals looked with favor upon President Kennedy's courting the independent-minded poet Robert Frost. Frost, before the largest audience a poet has ever had, honored Kennedy with a poem read from his Inaugural platform, and later spoke somewhat extravagantly of a coming age of power and poetry. Kennedy, for his part, paid a perceptive tribute to Frost. Frost had teased that "a liberal is someone who can't take his own side of an argument." Kennedy showed he understood and appreciated Frost's conservatism when the President said Robert Frost

> . . . will live as a poet of the darkness and despair, as well as the hope, which is, in his case, limited by a certain skepticism, and for his wit and understanding of man's limitations which lie beyond all man's profoundest statements.

More basic than Kennedy's direct appeal to writers was his display of certain qualities appreciated not only by intellectuals but by any serious liberal arts student. Paramount among these is the ability to learn from books—from the ideas and lives of other times and places—as well as from personal experience. American business and politics, and especially the road to the White House, have placed a premium upon learning from personal experience and from factual material. To many thoughtful persons a more complex age made it particularly appropriate for a president to combine gracefully vicarious literary experience with practical experience of public affairs. Parts of the Kennedy literature, and particularly some of the major biographies, make it clear that Kennedy did indeed incorporate into his life and decisions insights from books he had read and admired—

especially from English and American history and political biography.

Of course his major use of reading was to learn from contemporaries. Like Franklin D. Roosevelt, Kennedy was a "brain picker." But he could use reading to find the brains he needed to pick, and after talking with the writer he could go on reading for elaboration of the ideas the writer had to impart. Labor, defense, foreign policy, and the "new economics" are only a few of the policy areas he approached in this way. "What good are ideas unless you can make use of them?" Kennedy would habitually ask intellectuals. He sought aides who could summarize their thinking clearly and he often found a relationship between the ability to do this in written and verbal form. Sometimes Kennedy's favorable impression of an author's book or books would, along with other factors, encourage him to bring the author into his Administration—as with Arthur Schlesinger, Generals Gavin and Taylor, Richard Neustadt, and W. W. Rostow. Others, such as economist Paul Samuelson, would stay outside the Administration but continue to educate the President through memoranda, books, and conversation. As President Kennedy first settled into office, Professor John Morton Blum of Yale reported

> The recent works of his advisers, among others Richard E. Neustadt, Robert Triffin, Walt W. Rostow and Arthur Schlesinger, Jr., form a kind of reference library for his convictions and intentions.

Kennedy further held the attention of writers by his literary appreciation of a good phrase, whether his own or one borrowed. He could work into his speeches naturally sophisticated phrases which might have seemed pretentious if uttered by a Harding, Truman, Eisenhower, or Johnson. In illuminating aptness he was no match for the master craftsman of phrases Franklin D. Roosevelt, and the Kennedy wit, although pithy, only occasionally equaled Adlai Stevenson's best. Yet, with Kennedy as with Stevenson it was memorable phrases as much as general content which would make sizeable numbers of readers wish to possess volumes of their collected speeches and somewhat fewer go back to them for a second reading. If the words of either of these two men continue to educate readers a decade from now it will be in large part because certain of their phrases, handed down, illuminate, and lead the reader to, their larger ideas.

Kennedy summarized his whole attraction for young people in a phrase he said he derived from Greek philosophy:

> Happiness is the full use of your powers along lines of excellence in a life affording scope.

In a similar vein Kennedy would attempt to enlist youth in political life by quoting John Buchan, a favorite author-statesman who maintained "public life is the greatest and most honorable adventure."

But along with such exhortation he would occasionally call for a more practical understanding by drawing on another English statesman who admonished: "Politics is a field where action is one long second best, and where the choice constantly lies between two blunders." Later, when a guessing game erupted over responsibility for the military and political blunders at Cuba's Bay of Pigs, President Kennedy at a press conference, with apparent spontaneity, philosophized: "Victory has a hundred fathers, and defeat is an orphan." Or, as he wryly told a subsequent interviewer, "The President has the burden of responsibility. The advisers may move on to new advice."

Of course, Kennedy writers, like most other politicians' ghosts, plundered Bartlett's *Familiar Quotations,* but Kennedy's key and oft repeated quotations came from works he had read, admired, and understood. Thus his borrowed material had a certain coherence of attitude and fit into an overall Kennedy view of political life.

Sometimes as a Senator and aggressive presidential contender he used startling, almost macabre, Cassandra-like phrases, later largely dropped, reminding us that for a brief period he reputedly took phrases from comedian Mort Saul. Then, candidate Kennedy would tell a group of engineers that after hearing scientists give defense testimony in their detached, statistical manner, he believed there was a point to the wisecrack that "Life is extinct on other planets because their scientists were more advanced than ours." Or, Senator Kennedy would remark elsewhere, "We and the Russians have the power to destroy with one blow one quarter of the earth's population—a feat not accomplished since Cain slew Abel." These and related phrases about the "nuclear missile gap" constitute part of what Professor William G. Carleton, further along in this bibliography, criticizes as the highly alarmist nature of Kennedy's campaigning.

44 THE KENNEDY LITERATURE

Many of Kennedy's better phrases, however, were far less contrived and struck a deep chord of common sense. To a news conference questioner who complained about the unfairness of a military call up, President Kennedy bluntly replied, "Life is unfair. . . . Some people are sick, others are well." A President who never knew a day without back pain had established a bond with average people who quietly carry unexplainable private burdens.

While in Europe President Kennedy reminded his German listeners and others of the basic fact that "There are no permanent enemies." That this simple truth had to be uttered at all throws a light on the conditions of the age, but it also suggested new departures in policy. Another simple but significant foreign policy phrase, President Kennedy's statement at American University that his country seeks to "make the world safe for diversity," quickly won a more sympathetic hearing abroad than many more ideologically restrictive goals enunciated by previous administrations.

For intellectual listeners he could be more sophisticated—Arthur Schlesinger has boasted that Kennedy was the only person he knew who ever quoted Madam de Staël on "Meet the Press." Kennedy, in fact, even felt he could ask his intellectual betters for humility. The President addressed the forty-nine Nobel Prize winners whom he hosted as "the most extraordinary collection . . . of human knowledge that has ever gathered at the White House with the possible exception of when Thomas Jefferson dined alone."

The striking phrases of Kennedy's Inaugural Address are too well recalled to require comment, other than to note that the listener's fascination with their polish caused them to be more often quoted than analyzed or seriously thought through. American listeners and readers seem to have pondered very little the basic implications of an incoming President of a single country addressing the peoples in huts and villages around the world while virtually ignoring in the same address the conditions of his own country. Graceful phrasing also made it easy to overlook the speech's apparent internal contradictions concerning defense and the consequences of the arms race. There is no question, however, that the speech was a triumph of memorable phrases and exhortation for which President Kennedy will be long remembered.

Such phrases as those mentioned above still add occasional sparkle to the Kennedy literature and during Kennedy's lifetime they appealed strongly to the literary community. The obvious fact that Kennedy contributed no original thought and was a popularizer rather than a writer of the first rank seemed largely irrelevant to intellectuals as well as to the country at large. It was not characteristic of Americans of any calling to want or trust a high ranking official who was more the intellectual than the politician. But in Kennedy the characteristics and gestures just discussed combined with a mix of education, youth, experience, glamor, and public relations which built a meaningful bridge between the politician and serious writers.

Two of the consequences of his relationship to the world of writing are of special interest to those seeking to understand his period and his lingering impact. For one thing, writers' fascination with the distinctive style of John F. Kennedy helped exaggerate the reported substantial differences between the Eisenhower and Kennedy Administrations. The reader needs to use an unusually perceptive eye to discern the basic similarities. Another consequence was that writers' attachment to Kennedy, as being almost one of their own, made it all the more difficult for his successor to govern.

A minor irritation for readers stemming from writers' attitude toward Kennedy was the tendency of some writers to write as if they were whispering into the ear of the President rather than bringing the facts to their readers and letting the chips fall where they might. Sometimes writers overlooked failings they might have attacked in a less attractive man. The author of this bibliography, having once been set down in the rocker in Kennedy's Oval Office and told by a Kennedy worshipper that critics outside the White House could not know how difficult this good President's life was, is sensitive to how persuasive the Kennedy version of events could be.

The entire relationship of Kennedy to the world of arts and letters can be easily misunderstood. Even the admiring Sorensen records that "his respect for artistic excellence exceeded his appreciation." His wife once teased that the only tune he enjoyed was "Hail the Chief," and it is true that he liked drilling the Marine band on the White House grounds more than he enjoyed any symphony he ever attended. On Broadway his taste ran to run of the mill musicals and the films he saw were generally third rate "action" cinema. He was a beef steak and potatoes man who on the campaign trail fancied milk shakes.

Nevertheless, public figures can sometimes have an impact through gestures of interest and concern, and Kennedy—more precisely Kennedy and his wife—had a generally elevating influence on American taste. Kennedy's relation to the world of letters was undoubtedly deeper than his relation to other aspects of cultural life. Even so, a future generation may wonder at the strong sentimental attachment writers had for the young President. How else to explain the lament of Norman Mailer upon Kennedy's death: "For a while the country was ours. Now it's theirs again."

KENNEDY AND HIS BIOGRAPHERS

Both Sorensen and Schlesinger, along with other Kennedy aides, make a major point of the fact that Kennedy should have been, and would have been, the major Kennedy biographer. They testify to his objectivity, his awareness of implications of forces and events, and his proven ability as a historian, and agree that his own work would have surpassed the others. They also agree with Kennedy that only the President himself knows all the pressures which are operating on that office and only he can best say why a certain decision was ultimately made. Kennedy's "memoirs" in fact are one of the only Presidential memoirs to receive a review without having ever been written. Sorensen states

> He not only could measure his own performance but also cared deeply about how that performance would be measured by future historians as well as contemporary voters. His own recollection of public service would have made a memorable volume—carefully factual, amazingly frank, witty and wise—and none of the biographers can hope to do as well.

Kennedy, however, did not make adequate arrangements for writing the kind of convincing memoirs which he would have admired most. He did not keep a diary nor did he record his private observations of personalities or events, although he did occasionally dictate memoranda for files and, according to Sorensen, "he arranged for the comprehensive transcription of major deliberations." Evelyn Lincoln, who did keep her own diary, was aware that the President was having her file various copies of letters and documents for his memoirs. But we can expect to find no diaries or unpublished manuscripts of Kennedy himself.

Kennedy was particularly anxious that there should be a comprehensive White House record of events for comparison, since so many writers of ability he brought into his Administration were certain to have their comments upon events occurring during his term of office. Mrs. Lincoln recalls an order he asked her to relay to national security aide McGeorge Bundy, instructing him that the President "would like a copy of any memoranda, minutes, notes, and such which he might make for our files." It was Kennedy's understanding that the files of the National Security Council did not automatically become part of the White House files. "When I leave the White House," he told his secretary, "it would be helpful in reconstructing the record of the Administration to have that material in our files."

It is basically from such files and from the elaboration and interpretation his memory could give to them that Kennedy would have had to work. Sorensen recalls Kennedy asking him if he were sure he got down on paper a significant comment by a cabinet aide "for the book we're going to write," although Sorensen then, and on other occasions, said that he was filing material for the book the President alone was going to write. From available evidence, however, it seems likely that the writing-thinking relationship between Kennedy and Sorensen had become too fixed a feature of their intellectual lives for Kennedy to be willing to sever it: the memoirs probably would have been written with the aid of Sorensen. As it turned out, Sorensen had to work from the files on his own; what he deleted for security reasons or propriety (Sorensen's categories) may have been more than Kennedy would have felt necessary to omit.

It has already been mentioned that Kennedy was very particular about who wrote his biography and would try to prevent a biography which he believed would be biased or ill-informed. He believed, very often with justification, that inaccurate stories about him were simply repeated without verification and his statements often taken out of context. Kennedy was caustic in private about his most critical biographers; as for Victor Lasky's vitriolic *JFK: The Man and the Myth,* Sorensen reports that Kennedy "dismissed both book and author as more pitifully ridiculous than dangerous." But the President did read the book and briefed himself on it for press conferences. He seemed stung as he acknowledged to one questioner at a press conference that he had seen the Lasky book highly praised by Roscoe Drummond of the *New York Herald Tribune* and Arthur Krock of the *New York Times.* Those columnists had, in fact, only pointed out that this book would serve as a partial antidote to all the praise which Kennedy had been receiving.

When at the same press conference Kennedy was asked if he did not consider *Time* Magazine White House reporter Hugh Sidey's friendly book, *John F. Kennedy, President,* too uncritical, he replied that he did not consider it uncritical at all. Sorensen tells us Kennedy "continually befriended, chastised and sought to enlighten" Sidey (in the subsequent Johnson Administration, this would be referred to as "the treatment"); indeed, Kennedy considered Sidey much more fair and accurate than the publication which he served. In an attempt to overcome what he considered *Time's* bias, Kennedy appealed directly to Henry Luce and even reminded him that Luce publications paid in postage less than 40 per cent of the cost of mail handling, while the Federal government provided the rest.

Kennedy's dissatisfaction with Burns' sympathetic, but unyieldingly objective biography, *John Kennedy: A Political Profile,* was anticipated by the author. At the front of his work, Burns dedicated "To John Kennedy" a poem by the Scottish poet Robert Burns, which expresses the sadness of the biographer who wished to be both friendly and objective with Kennedy. It read:

> . . . But if, as I'm informéd weel,
> Ye hate as ill's the vera Deil
> The flinty heart that canna feel —
>   Come sir, here's tae you!
> Hae, there's my han', I wiss you weel,
>   An' Gude be wi' you!"
>
> Robert Burns, 1786

Kennedy made it quite clear that biographer Burns had failed to emphasize properly the enormous growth in Kennedy's later career, the essence of which Burns had indeed recorded, but which the professor saw in somewhat smaller proportion to the overall picture than did Kennedy. Sorensen, as a defender of the President against all detractors, notes Kennedy's feeling that Burns believed "unless somebody overstates or shouts at the top of their voice they are not concerned about a matter." Kennedy's irritation with Burns was, we are told, even shared by the President's wife. Sorensen flatly states that Kennedy chose Burns as an unofficial biographer "because he believed Burns' ability, and his standing in the liberal community, would give the book stature among the audience we hoped it would reach." Some conflict between the aims of the biographer and those of his subject was certain to develop.

Kennedy certainly knew when he took Schlesinger into his White House staff that this distinguished historian of the Franklin Roosevelt era would someday write a history of the Administration in which he took part. Kennedy had solid respect for Schlesinger's volumes on Roosevelt and asked many questions about how and why Roosevelt handled one or another situation. For Kennedy in the White House, Schlesinger was the main link to the outside intellectual community. Even if Schlesinger was not, as Mrs. Evelyn Lincoln makes pointedly clear, a real Kennedy insider—which forced Schlesinger to rely on secondhand information more than he might have wished—the President felt real affection for him and they understood each other well. Nevertheless, Schlesinger's position in the White House was not too secure at first. At the start of the Administration, Schlesinger remarks that Kennedy said he did not want his staff recording the daily discussions in the White House; the President must, after all, have the privilege of thinking out loud and of making flippant or even harsh remarks under the strain of irritation, without the fear of being quoted out of context. Kennedy mentioned, as a case in point, an inclusion in the Morgenthau diaries of some of Franklin Roosevelt's jokes during a crisis. Some readers might have a similar reaction to Sorensen's quoting Kennedy during the Cuban missile crisis, during which the President teased about who would be left out of the overcrowded White House air raid shelters if worse came to worst.

Partly because of a friendly warning by Margaret Truman, but even more because of his own experience in an immensely wealthy and servant-overloaded family, Kennedy forbade his household servants to write of their White House experiences. This ban, however, did not apply to his coworkers in the Administration who had to await his spoken guidelines on how much they should record or publish. Nonetheless, even with aides Kennedy had some reserve and mentioned to more than one of them that generally he had little confidence in memoirs of aides of previous administrations.

Kennedy also specifically complained about Emmet Hughes's using Eisenhower's confidences as ammunition against Ike in Hughes' *Ordeal of Power*. What Hughes did was to point out that within the Eisenhower Administration there was always talk about new departures in policies, but they never came to anything; a similar work by a White House insider would contribute much to a more balanced picture of the Kennedy Administration.

In the light of Kennedy's restrictive guidelines, Schlesinger kept only fragmentary notations in his diary during the first weeks of the Administration. But with the Bay of Pigs failure, Kennedy coined what he christened an "old saying": "Victory has a hundred fathers and defeat is an orphan." He recognized the need for a White House version of historical events, and accordingly, told Schlesinger he hoped his aide had kept a full record of the Bay of Pigs developments. Schlesinger's diaries became infinitely more adequate after Kennedy said,

> No, you go ahead. You can be damn sure that the CIA has its record and the Joint Chiefs theirs. We'd better make sure we have a record over here.

In general the biographies of Kennedy as President by Sorensen and Schlesinger are in keeping with the canons of biography which Kennedy set for himself. While the other memoirs written to date by Kennedy's intimates are not as comprehensive or thorough in their analyses as these two major works, they would also seem to fall within the standards Kennedy found acceptable.

There is a large and varied enough readership in the country to accommodate almost any point of view, but ultimately the standing of a man rests with all the people who remember him. In a Gallup poll completed just prior to his death, the public described President Kennedy as "intelligent, dedicated, likeable, cultured, attractive, dynamic, friendly, and confident." To this was soon added their appreciation of a young leader who died in the service of his country. It is against this background that all the writing about John Fitzgerald Kennedy has been launched.

CHAPTER I.

Kennedy's Writing

Kennedy, John F., "My Brother Joe", in Kennedy, John F., ed. *As We Remember Joe,* Cambridge, Mass.: Privately Printed at the University Press, 1945, pp. 1–5.

This seventy-five page book of remembrances and tributes to Kennedy's older brother Joseph P. Kennedy, Jr., is of major interest to those studying the sociology of the Kennedy family and to that part of the Kennedy legend concerned with the passing of the torch from the father to his eldest son. The contributors include members of his family, friends, and associates. The family's ambition to move beyond money to the highest level of public service seems to have settled on the eldest surviving son. In his tribute to Joe Jr., killed in the war, Professor Harold Laski of the London School of Economics wrote: "He often sat in my study and submitted, with that smile that was pure magic, to relentless teasing about his determination to be nothing less than President of the United States." Writing about his brother in his book, John said, "I think if the Kennedy children ever amount to anything, it will be due more to Joe's behavior and his conduct than to any other factor." As a Senator, Kennedy later told a reporter that he had taken over when Joe Jr. was killed and Robert would take his place in the Senate if anything happened to him. Kennedy's most sympathetic biographers mention this remark, but omit the fact that during Kennedy's first senatorial campaign, 900,000 copies of a tabloid were distributed showing Kennedy the war hero. The tabloid included photos and story of Joe Jr. under the headline: "John Fulfills Dream of Brother Joe Who Met Death in the Skies Over the English Channel." The eldest son tradition, it should be noted, still continues.

As early as 1957, a *Saturday Evening Post* reporter wrote that Kennedy backers in Massachusetts "confidently look forward to the day when Jack will be in the White House, Bobby will serve in the Cabinet as Attorney General and Teddy will be Senator from Massachusetts." *As We Remember Joe,* of which only 500 copies were printed, must now be sought in the rare book rooms of libraries and an autographed copy of it has brought thousands of dollars at auction.

Kennedy, John F. *Why England Slept.* **New York: Wilfred Funk, Inc., 1940, 252 pp. Introduction by Henry Luce. Reissued 1961, with new introduction by Henry Luce. Paperback ed., New York: Dolphin Books, 1961. 200 pp.**

This is the development into book form of the twenty-three-year-old Kennedy's senior honors thesis in government at Harvard. The thesis was entitled "Appeasement at Munich" and was done under the direction of Professors Bruce Hopper and Payson Wilde (John Wheeler Bennet is another person thanked in the preface of the book for his suggestions). The thesis is deposited in the Widner Library, Harvard University. Kennedy, who had just returned from a semester's traveling in Europe, seeks to find the reasons behind the Munich Pact and World War II which followed. The pact, he argues, was the result of low British morale and of the condition of her armaments which made "surrender" inevitable.

In this book, Kennedy develops to some extent a few ideas which guide his thinking throughout his life. The struggle between "hard" and "soft" societies, for example, is explored. Another idea dealt with is that of the difficulties of democracies to adjust to the challenge of aggressive foreign dictatorships. Still other ideas include the central relationship of armaments to diplomacy and the need to be ready to fight when challenged.

The relevancy of these ideas to later problems of guerilla insurgency confronting Kennedy's Presidency is obvious. In a speech made after the Cuban missile crisis had subsided, Kennedy declared:

> The complacent, the self-indulgent, the soft societies are about to be swept away with the debris of history. Only the strong, only the industrious, only the determined, only the courageous, only the visionary who determined the real nature of the struggle can possibly survive. . . . Too long we have fixed our eyes on traditional military needs, on armies prepared to cross borders, on missiles poised for flight. Now it should be clear that this is no longer enough—that our security may be lost piece by piece, country by country, without the firing of a single missile or the crossing of a single border. . . . We intend to intensify our efforts for a struggle in many ways more difficult than war, where disappointment will often accompany us.

Burns develops some evidence that, as a result of correspondence with his father, Ambassador Kennedy, the young author shifted a small part of the blame for Munich from impersonal forces, ranging from economics, party politics, pacifism, and an apathetic public, to the mistakes of leaders in the British government. He chastized Prime Minister Stanley Baldwin and praised Winston Churchill, whom he saw as rousing England from her slumber. Despite these ventures into personalities, Kennedy held to his basic contention that unless these impersonal forces were altered (and he says little about how they can be other than through strong leadership) there is not much the leader can do when the crunch comes.

Some phrases in *Why England Slept* ring like recent history. A month before the Cuban missile crisis, I pointed out in a personal conversation with a Soviet diplomat the following passages from the President's early book. I do not know whether he took them seriously, although they would have been instructive. "We must," wrote Kennedy,

> keep our armaments equal to our commitments. Munich should teach us that; we must realize that our bluff will be called. We cannot tell anyone to stay out of our hemisphere unless armaments and the people behind those armaments are prepared to back up the command, even to the ultimate point of going to war. There must be no doubt in anyone's mind, the decision must be automatic: if we debate, if we hesitate, if we question, it will be too late.

In his first introduction to this work, publisher Henry R. Luce reflected upon the perennial adult worry that the younger generation is going to the dogs. "If John F. Kennedy is characteristic of this generation—and I believe he is—many of us would be happy to have the destiny of this Republic handed over to his generation at once." Luce had second thoughts by 1960, but he was nevertheless proud to write a second, and considerably less excited, introduction for the 1961 reissue of *Why England Slept*.

The critical reader will be impressed with the fantastic degree to which the post World War II politicians and statesmen, Kennedy among them, have lived intellectually off reading the Munich tea leaves. Critics of the traditional "balance of power" politics offer another interpretation of the significance of Munich: The national state is no longer a safe instrument with which to conduct international affairs. If this alternate view is ultimately correct and Kennedy misinterpreted Munich, then this book stressing the need for a strong, sovereign state is all the more important, since it remained Kennedy's intellectual anchor on the question.

Kennedy, John F. "War in Indochina," *Vital Speeches,* May 1954, pp. 418–24.

This contains the substance of the first Senate speech John F. Kennedy gave on the fateful subject of Vietnam, a country he had visited in 1951. Like many other liberal Americans he was quick to criticize French colonial errors in Indochina as well as in Algeria, but seemed little to realize that America might not be immune to similar problems and criticisms as it took over responsibilities in Vietnam. In this speech Kennedy argued for an end to French colonialism in Vietnam and spoke against unilateral American intervention, warning of Asian hostility to it and the military trap involved. He repeated this theme in an article "What should the U. S. Do in Indochina?" *Foreign Policy Bulletin,* May 15, 1954, pp. 4–6, but became bouyantly, probably even naively enthusiastic about America's ability to help bring social welfare and democracy to Ngo Dinh Diem's regime. This latter sentiment was expressed in a speech before the American Friends of Vietnam, June 1, 1956, contained in his collection of speeches entitled *The Strategy of Peace*.

President Johnson's claim to have basically continued Kennedy's

Vietnam policies is a very complex claim. An evaluation of it requires a careful reading of relevant sections of works cited in this bibliography by Sorensen, Schlesinger, and Hilsman, as well as Kennedy's press conferences. President Johnson's claims are set forth in a number of his speeches and press conferences. Before he became actively engaged in a contest with Johnson for the Presidency, the clearest challenge by Robert Kennedy to Johnson's claim was in an interview reported in the *New York Times,* November 27, 1967, the story entitled "Kennedy Asserts Johnson Shifted U.S. Aim in Vietnam." On the same date in this newspaper, John Herbers presented a résumé of conflicting evidence in an article entitled "President Kennedy's Vietnam Aim Debated Again." It is a complicated question, but one subject to fruitful research, even without access to classified documents.

Kennedy, John F. *Profiles in Courage.* **New York: Harper & Brothers, 1956, 266 pp. Paperback ed., with a Special Foreword by Robert F. Kennedy, New York: Harper & Row, 1964. 283 pp.**

This book, written during more than one year's convalescence, is chiefly concerned with the experiences of eight United States Senators who risked their political careers in supporting a cause they thought just but whose constituencies did not. Among the eight Senators are John Quincy Adams, Daniel Webster, Thomas Hart Benton, Sam Houston, Edmund G. Ross, Lucius Quintus Cincinnatus Lamar, George Norris, and Robert A. Taft.

Adams incurred the wrath of the Federalists in his party for supporting measures of Thomas Jefferson, the man who had defeated his father for the Presidency. Webster's anti-slavery constituents were enraged when the Senator from Massachusetts spoke in support of Henry Clay's Compromise of 1850, which provided that slavery, where it already existed, should remain. Benton, the Senator from slave-holding Missouri, enraged his pro-slavery constituents by not speaking in support of the same Compromise in 1850. Houston lost his seat in the Senate for aligning himself with Benton and other pro-Union Senators, and later the Governorship of the state when he refused to support Texas' vote for secession. Ross, to the dismay of *his* constituents, cast the deciding vote against impeachment of President Andrew Johnson.

In an attempt to promote a spirit of harmony within the recently united country, Lamar of Mississippi had scorn heaped upon him for eulogizing Charles Sumner, the radical Republican who had "helped make the Reconstruction a black nightmare the South could never forget." The Republican Norris, against the wishes of his constituency, opposed America's entrance into World War I and supported Catholic Democrat Alfred Smith for the Presidency. Taft risked an embittered constituency by challenging the legality of the post-World War II Nuremberg Trials.

Despite the seriousness of this book, it is fun to read. One comes away from *Profiles in Courage* feeling that the temporary cripple who wrote it was amusing himself by describing the mayhem of roughhouse politics, which Kennedy enjoyed vicariously, but tried to stand above. Kennedy agreed with Ernest Hemingway that a good definition of courage was "grace under pressure," although several of the heroes and many of their critics whom Kennedy discussed in his book were not only graceless but more courageous and interesting for want of grace. Kennedy quotes Houston: " 'The people want excitement and I had as well give it as anyone.' " Plenty of excitement *was* provided; Houston peeled "off his shirt during the hot summer campaign, harangued audiences in every corner of Texas with his great fund of vituperative epithets and withering sarcasm."

Furthermore, as Kennedy noted, a newspaper critic called Houston's speeches "a compound of abuses and egotism . . . without the sanction of historical truth . . . it was characterized from beginning to end by such epithets as fellow thieves, rascals, and assassins."

Andrew Johnson, another hero of Kennedy, while still a Senator, made a trip home to persuade his state to remain in the Union. He was stopped in Virginia by an angry mob which "dragged the Senator from his car, assaulted and abused him, and decided not to lynch him only at the last minute, with the rope around his neck," when they agreed that hanging was the privilege of his neighbors in Tennessee. Senator Benton of Missouri, Kennedy tells us, "ransacked the entire English language for terms of scorn and derision." Another Senator, Ross, was described by a critic quoted by Kennedy as a "poor, pitiful, shriveled wretch, with a soul so small that a little pelf would outweigh all things else that dignify or ennoble manhood."

Each of the book's chapters is rather short and the text is lightened with unexpected anecdotes and occasional wit. Kennedy's ideas on the subject of courage are best exemplified in the opening chapter on "Courage and Politics" and the closing one "The Meaning of Courage." See also the section "Who Wrote *Profiles in Courage?*" in the Introduction to this bibliography.

Kennedy, John F. "Democrat Says Party Must Lead or Get Left," *Life,* March 11, 1957, pp. 16–44.

This piece best elaborated Kennedy's belief that parties had to stand for something and had to be modern in organization, method, and personnel in order to attract and hold majorities in the mid-twentieth century. In this article his published words come closest to matching the harsh private judgment he made of old line Democratic party "hacks." Some of the ideas expressed here underlay Kennedy's penchant for building a personal political organization parallel to the regular Democratic organization, a practice which may have long-range implications for American political campaigning.

Kennedy, John F., "A Message to You from the White House," *Life,* September 15, 1961, p. 95.

A reminder of the alarmist nature of Kennedy's reaction to his encounter with Krushchev in Vienna, the President stressed the immediate urgency of private and public fallout shelters. His appeal by and large fell on deaf ears and he later radically, if quietly, scaled down his campaign for fallout shelters.

Kennedy, John F., "A Democrat Looks at Foreign Policy," *Foreign Affairs,* October, 1957, pp. 44–59.

This judicious piece carried in one of the most prestigious American journals did perhaps more than anything else written by Kennedy at the time to convince influential people of various political persuasions that he should be taken seriously as a thinker on foreign policy. While Kennedy was generally safe and responsible in his political thinking, he was imaginative enough to have settled on a few breakthroughs which comfortably could be made, and called for a few discarded practices which should have been revived. He argued that ambassadors such as Chester Bowles and John Sherman Cooper should be appointed again; bipartisanship should be restored and Republican advisers like John J. McCloy of the Chase Manhattan Bank and Robert Lovett should again serve a Democratic President. Interestingly, while many liberals thought Kennedy would appoint Chester Bowles Secretary of State, he instead did what is hinted here: he offered Lovett the job, and, upon his refusal, offered it to Dean Rusk. In addition, Kennedy made McCloy his chief disarmament aide and sent Bowles to India as ambassador.

In the article, Kennedy takes a swing at the self-righteousness of John Foster Dulles and neatly catches contemplative Adlai Stevenson in the backswing: "If Don Quixote is a poor inspiration for the makers of foreign policy so, too, is Hamlet."

Here, as elsewhere, Kennedy is hopelessly confused about Asia. "Our current and increasingly successful policy in Indochina," he writes, "never a strong feature of the State Department under either Republican or Democratic control, has its origin in Congress." For those who wish to change the Cold War, he places partial blame upon State Department rigidity, charging that however hard the Soviets may be, "we delude ourselves if we believe that on this account we are more maneuverable and flexible in our action."

Kennedy took pride in this article and he responded to a comment made by me about it by sending me a long telegram.

Kennedy, John F., "The Voter's Choice in the Bay State. A Review of Joseph Huthmacher's *Massachusetts Peoples and Politics 1919–1933*,**" New York Book Review, September 20, 1959, p. 42.**

Murray Kempton writes that Kennedy spoke of the Boston Irish very much the way his hero, Lord Melbourne, spoke of the Irish of Dublin. This may be slightly overstated, but considering Kennedy's origins, his professorial aloofness from his forebears is impressive. Kennedy did not write much about Boston; thus this review of a Georgetown University professor's book on that city's politics is of more than ordinary interest. In the course of the review, Kennedy pays tribute to the progressive Republicans Massachusetts has produced, including Henry Cabot Lodge, Jr., Leverett Saltonstall, Christian Herter, and Sinclair Weeks.

"Honey Fitz" would undoubtedly have gagged.

Kennedy, John F., "Books in the News," Review of H. Lindell Hart's *Deterrent or Defense, Saturday Review,* September 3, 1960, p. 17.

How Kennedy found time to read and review a book during his hectic Presidential campaign period is not made clear, but the words sound like his own. Kennedy summarizes Hart's view in these words: "Keep strong if possible. In any case, keep cool. Have unlimited patience. Never corner an opponent and always assist him to save face. Avoid self-righteousness like the devil—nothing is so self-blinding."

This review is further evidence of his very great interest in military strength as a bargaining point in disarmament negotiations. He shows keen awareness both here and in *The Strategy of Peace* of the changes nuclear weapons have brought.

Kennedy, John F. *The Strategy of Peace.* Edited by Allan Nevins. New York: Harper and Brothers, 1960. 233 pp. Also available in an identical paperback edition.

In his introduction to this book, historian Allan Nevins, formerly a Stevenson man, invited the reader to see that it is now Kennedy who is "talking sense to the American people" on foreign affairs.

Indeed, *The Strategy of Peace,* which includes Kennedy's speeches from the late 1950's up to the summer of 1960, did much to convince persons who wanted new departures in foreign policy that they *could* transfer their hopes from Stevenson to the young Bostonian. The speeches are a result of Kennedy's wide reading and his conversations with some of the better informed minds in government and the universities. Most of the speeches were drafted in collaboration with Sorensen, although working papers and suggestions for content and subject matter were offered by others, among them John Kenneth Galbraith of Harvard, Walt W. Rostow of M.I.T., fellow Democrat Chester Bowles, and, from the Republican side, Senator John Sherman Cooper, former Ambassador to India.

The speeches, unfortunately, contain inadequately examined hopes: first, that the United States could enhance its armed might and at the same time achieve a significant beginning of disarmament; second, that the nation could expand the military establishment yet increase civil liberties; third, that the country could encourage basic social revolution abroad which would not interfere with American foreign investments; and finally, that America could influence events on a global scale without reaping some of the ambiguous rewards involved; for instance, in its attempt to install democracy in South Vietnam without inheriting an odious imperialistic stigma. Kennedy was much too inclined to believe that it was Eisenhower, and not America itself, who had made it impossible for the country to provide creative world leadership and to employ constructive social policies abroad. America, thought Kennedy, must not land the Marines anytime there was social change in Latin America of which we disapproved. In addition, the United States must not be maneuvered into a catastrophic land war in Asia. One of Kennedy's firmest and most idealistic beliefs was that the United States had much in common with the masses of mankind and could even help speed their social revolutions. As it turned out, much of the book proved embarrassing to the orator once he reached the White House and Kennedy's relatively small reservoir of irritation was spent liberally on those who pointedly asked whatever became of those specific hopes.

For readers who choose to pursue the fascinating and as yet unsettled question of whether Kennedy's very effective, vote-getting use of the "missile gap" and the "economic gap" issues was a result of misinformation or of incredible opportunism, considerable evidence is offered in these speeches. (Both "gaps" disappeared almost as soon as Kennedy came to the White House.)

At the close of the book is a most high-level and fascinating discussion of future American foreign policy between John Fischer, editor-in-chief of *Harper's* Magazine, and Senator Kennedy. Kennedy's extemporaneous remarks to Fischer are intelligent and, for the most part, quite clear; his knowledge of the subject under discussion is well-digested, not just "rehearsed," and his grasp of the pertinent issues is most impressive. Upon reading it, even his most vehement detractors would have to admit that even if he couldn't write a fine book, he could certainly dictate one.

For all its unexamined premises, *The Strategy of Peace* contains many illuminating flashes of brilliance and remains the most intellectually provocative work which bears the Kennedy name.

Kennedy, John F. *To Turn the Tide: A Selection from President Kennedy's Public Statements from his Election Through the 1961 Adjournment of Congress, Setting Forth the Goals of his*

First Legislative Year. Edited by John W. Gardner. Foreword by Carl Sandburg. Introduction by President John F. Kennedy. New York: Harper and Brothers, 1962. 235 pp. Paperback ed., New York: Popular Library, 1962. 212 pp.

This is a readily available source of some of the main policy statements of the early months of the Kennedy Administration. The editor emphasizes Kennedy's preoccupation with foreign affairs, and celebrates Kennedy's "extraordinary capacity to express himself in speech and writing." Amidst rambling and unqualified praise, poet Sandburg offers one solid comment: Kennedy's speeches rank in content, substance, and style with those of Jefferson, Lincoln, Wilson, and the two Roosevelts. Kennedy's own introduction frankly and engagingly admits the limitations of Presidential statements. First, he says wryly, "We live in an age when the conduct of foreign affairs consists of more than 'open covenants openly arrived at.' " Also, the President's words, especially on foreign policy, "are certain to be heard and likely to be acted upon by more than one audience: adversaries, allies, neutrals, the Congress, and other members of the Administration as well as all the diverse individuals and interest groups which compose the American electorate. Each must be taken into account."

This collection contains Kennedy's impressive "Speech to the Massachusetts State Legislature" (Jan. 9, 1961), his brilliant Inaugural Address with its challenging internal contradictions relating to the armaments race, and his excellent first "State of the Union Message" (Jan. 29, 1961), all of which are printed unabridged. On the negative side, the collection exposes Kennedy's extremely muddled thinking on his various proposals for Civil Defense measures and the remarkable degree to which he soft-peddled civil rights and unemployment during this period. Many of the documents are so abbreviated that they serve only to alert the reader to look elsewhere for their more complete texts. Kennedy's own hand can be much more clearly seen in the composition of the major speeches than in the messages to Congress which were largely prepared by Administrative aides. Sorensen's contribution to the speeches is, as usual, considerable.

Kennedy, John F. *The Burden and the Glory: The Hopes and Purposes of President Kennedy's Second and Third Years in Office as Revealed in His Published Statements and Ad-*

dresses. Edited by Allan Nevins. Foreword by President Lyndon B. Johnson. New York: Harper & Row, 1964. 293 pp.

This book is a useful source for the major Kennedy statements after *To Turn the Tide.* The most interesting speech is his major address on racial injustice, in which he committed himself, as never before, to a minority cause. Of great importance, to those who believe Kennedy had a sincere interest in pursuit of disarmament after his more fundamental efforts to keep America strongly armed, are his American University Address and his television speech on the Nuclear Test Ban Treaty. His *"Ich bin ein Berliner"* speech, which guaranteed his popularity in West Germany, steadied German confidence and, Kennedy hoped, would give him more maneuvering power in dealing with the Soviets, is also here.

Included in this collection is the speech which Kennedy was to have made at the Dallas Trade Mart on the day of the assassination, and which some Texas newspapers had already printed in their afternoon editions. In this speech Kennedy was forcefully to attack voices he heard in the land

> preaching doctrines wholly unrelated to reality . . . doctrines which apparently assume that words will suffice without weapons, that vituperation was as good as victory and that peace is a sign of weakness.

We cannot expect, Kennedy was to say,

> that everyone, to use the phrase of a decade ago, will 'talk sense to the American people.' But we can hope that fewer people will listen to nonsense. And the notion that this nation is headed for defeat through deficit or that strength is but a matter of slogans, is nothing but just plain nonsense.

He fell a few miles short of the platform from which this appeal to reason was to be delivered.

Kennedy, John F. *America the Beautiful, In the Words of John F. Kennedy.* Edited by the editors of *Country Beautiful Magazine,* Elm Grove, Wisconsin: Country Beautiful Foundation. Distributed by Doubleday, Inc., 1964. 80 pp.

Few such books of this type are included in this bibliography, but this particular collection of quotations and photos is so well chosen that some readers may undoubtedly wish to read or possess it. Most of it can be said to be an elaboration on the theme of Kennedy's Introduction to Stuart Udall's book on conservation, *The Quiet Crisis*. Kennedy there stated,

> I look forward to an America which will not be afraid of grace and beauty . . . and I look forward to an America which commands respect throughout the world not only for its strength but for its civilization as well.

Kennedy's concern with domestic matters and with America beyond the Eastern seaboard is brought out more clearly here than elsewhere.

Kennedy, John F. *A Nation of Immigrants.* **Introduction by Robert F. Kennedy. New York: Harper & Row, 1964. 160 pp. Paperback ed., New York: Popular Library, 1964. 160 pp.**

This was originally a pamphlet published in 1958 by the Anti-Defamation League of B'nai B'rith. It is written for the average layman although it may have been intended by Kennedy to persuade his fellow congressmen to support the amendments liberalizing the immigration law that he was sponsoring. In his introduction to the book, Robert Kennedy indicates that when the President sent a message to Congress urging a more complete and broader revision of immigration laws he had decided to revise the book, "for use as a weapon of enlightenment in the coming legislative battle." This revision was precluded by the President's death. In its present form, *A Nation of Immigrants* provides a general survey of the contributions of some of the varied immigrant groups in America, their problems, and the need for revisions of legislative policy. That such a need was obvious is pointed out by Kennedy when he discusses the Immigration and Nationality Act then in existence. He calls the Act quite inadequate, if only because of the tremendous number of private immigration bills introduced into Congress each session. These private bills, wrote Kennedy,

> deal with individual hardship cases for which the general law fails to provide. Private immigration bills make up about half of our legislation!

The book's tone is set when Kennedy asks America to avoid what the Irish poet John Boyle O'Reille called "Organized charity, scrimped and iced/In the name of a cautious, statistical Christ." The work includes a useful chronology of immigration waves to America and a center section of photographs of typical late nineteenth-century and early twentieth-century immigrants from Europe and Asia.

Kennedy, John F. *Public Papers of Presidents, 1961–1963.* National Archives and Records Service. Washington, D.C., 1962, 1963, 1964.

These volumes, issued annually, contain the Presidential proclamations, messages, and reports to Congress, as well as important public speeches and statements. The collection of speeches annotated earlier contain excerpts from the most important of these papers as well as speeches not contained in the Public Papers.

Kennedy, John F. *Memorable Quotations of John F. Kennedy.* Compiled by Maxwell Meyerson. New York: Thomas Y. Crowell, 1965. 314 pp.

This is the most complete and useful compendium of Kennedy quotations.

CHRONOLOGICAL LISTING OF ALL PUBLISHED WRITING ATTRIBUTED TO JOHN F. KENNEDY

The following chronological list represents the complete works attributed to John F. Kennedy contained in the Library of Congress and recorded in pertinent bibliographies and indexes. He is not known to have left any unpublished manuscripts intended for publication, other than government documents.

1940

Why England Slept. New York: W. Funk, 1940. 252 pp.

1945

New York Journal American (and other Hearst newspapers). Kennedy by-line articles on San Francisco Conference: April

28, 30; May 2, 3, 4, 5, 7, 9, 10, 14, 16, 18, 19, 21, 23, 28. From London on the British election June 24; July 10, 27; all 1945.

"My Brother Joe," in Kennedy, John Fitzgerald, ed. *As We Remember Joe.* Cambridge, Mass. Priv. print.: University Press, 1945, pp. 1–5.

1947

"Supplemental Minority Report." In U.S. Congress. House. Committee on Education and Labor. Labor-Management Relations Act, 1947, *Report.* 80th Cong. 1st. Sess. House. Report 245. Washington, D.C. pp. 113–15.

1949

"Need for Revision of Policy on Airline Competition and Mail Subsidy," *Congressional Digest.* January, 1949, pp. 28, 30.

1951

"How Should Cadets be Picked?" *New York Times Magazine,* August 19, 1951, pp. 16 ff.

1952

"The Case for Home Rule for Washington," *Congressional Digest,* December, 1952, pp. 304, 306.

1953

"Floor Beneath Wages is Gone," *New Republic,* July 20, 1953, pp. 14–15.

"What's Wrong with Social Security," *American Magazine,* October, 1953, pp. 109–12. "What's the Matter in New England?" *New York Times Magazine,* November 8, 1953, pp. 12 ff.

1954

"New England and the South," *Atlantic Monthly,* January, 1954, pp. 32–36.

"Social Security; Constructive if Not Bold," *New Republic,* February 8, 1954, pp. 14–15.

"War in Indo China," *Vital Speeches,* May 1, 1954, pp. 418–24.

"What Should the U.S. Do in Indo-China?" *Foreign Policy Bulletin,* May 15, 1954, pp. 4–6.

"Foreign Policy is the People's Business," *New York Times Magazine,* August 8, 1954, pp. 5 ff.

1955

"Great Day in American History," *Colliers,* November 25, 1955, pp. 40 ff. (Re: Daniel Webster).

"Ross of Kansas," *Harper's Magazine,* December, 1955, pp. 40–44.

"Challenge of Political Courage," *New York Times Magazine,* December 18, 1955, pp. 13 ff.

1956

Profiles in Courage. New York: Harper and Brothers, 266 pp.

"Statement on U.S. Immigration Policy," *Congressional Digest,* January, 1956, pp. 18, 20.

"To Keep the Lobbyist in Bounds," *New York Times Magazine,* February 19, 1956, pp. 11 ff.

"Brothers I Presume?" *Vogue,* April 1, 1956, pp. 117, 142.

"Take the Academies out of Politics," *Saturday Evening Post,* June 2, 1956, pp. 36 ff.

"America's Stake in Vietnam," *Vital Speeches,* August 1, 1956.

1957 *

"The Intellectual and the Politician," in *Representative American Speeches,* 1956–1957. New York: W. H. Wilson Co., 1957, pp. 165–72.

"Unemployment: How Government Will Help: Interview with John F. Kennedy," *U.S. News and World Report,* January 11, 1957, p. 133.

"Comity and Common Sense in the Middle East," *Vital Speeches,* April 1, 1957, pp. 359–61.

---

* Biographer James MacGregor Burns notes several Kennedy articles, presumably published in 1957, which the author of this bibliography has been unable to locate. They will probably be made available with other Kennedy records from his Senate period, with the opening of the Kennedy Library. These are: "What My Illness Taught Me," written for *American Weekly,* an article on brotherhood for *Parade,* and unspecified "pieces in business and labor periodicals."

"Democrat Says Party Must Lead or Get Left," *Life,* March 11, 1957, pp. 164 ff.

"Should U.S. Give Aid to Communist Countries?" letter, *Foreign Policy Bulletin,* April 15, 1957, p. 117.

"Search for the Five Greatest Senators," *New York Times Magazine,* April 14, 1957, pp. 14 ff.

"Education of an American Politician: Excerpts from an Address. *National Parent Teacher,* May, 1957, pp. 10–12.

"Profession of Politics," *Vital Speeches,* August 15, 1957, pp. 657–59.

"Let the Lady Hold up Her Head: Reflections on the American Immigration Policy." New York: American Jewish Committee, 1957, 7 pp.

"A Democrat Looks at Foreign Policy," *Foreign Affairs,* October, 1957, pp. 44–59. Also in Jacobson, Harold K., ed. *America's Foreign Policy.* New York: Random House, 1960, pp. 349–64.

"Algerian Crisis: A New Phase?" *America,* October 5, 1957, pp. 15–17.

1958

Good Fences Make Good Neighbors. Convocation Address. Frederickton, N.B.: University of New Brunswick. 1960. 11 pp.

"A Nation of Immigrants." New York: Anti-Defamation League, 1958. 40 pp. (One Nation Library).

"Portraits of Five Senators in the Senate Reception Room." In *Representative American Speeches:* 1957–58. New York: H.W. Wilson Co., 1958, pp. 83–95.

"Fate of the Nation," *NEA Journal,* January, 1958, pp. 10–11.

"If India Fails," *Progressive,* January, 1958, pp. 8–11.

"Three Women of Courage," *McCall's,* January, 1958, pp. 36 ff. (re: Jeanette Rankin, Anne Hutchinson, and Prudence Crandall.)

"Shame of the States," *New York Times Magazine,* May 18, 1958, pp. 12 ff.

"Spirit of One Man's Independence," *Reader's Digest,* July, 1958, pp. 104–05 (re: John Adams).

"When the Executive Fails to Lead," *Reporter,* September 18, 1958, pp. 14–17.

"General Gavin Sounds the Alarm," *Reporter,* October 30, 1958, pp. 35–36.

"The National Broadcasting Company Presents Senator John F. Kennedy," *Meet the Press.* Washington, D.C.: National Publishing Co., 1958. 9 pp.

1959

"Should the Kennedy Minimum Wage Proposal Be Adopted?" *Congressional Digest,* February, 1959, pp. 44 ff.

"Should Congress Re-enact the Vetoed Douglas Bill for New Federal Aid to Depressed Areas?" *Congressional Digest,* February, 1959, pp. 54 ff.

"Should Restrictions Against Secondary Boycott and Organizational Picketing be Strengthened?" *Congressional Digest,* August, 1959, pp. 203 ff.

"Labor Racketeers and Political Pressure," *Look,* May 12, 1959, pp. 17–21.

1960

The Strategy of Peace. Edited by Allan Nevins. New York: Harper and Brothers. 1960. 233 pp.

"Should Congress Retain the Loyalty Provisions of the N.D.E.A.?" *Congressional Digest,* April, 1960.

"Presidential Race Will Test a Very Great Unspoken Issue," *Alabama Municipal Journal,* January, 1960, pp. 5–7 (re: problems of the cities).

"Why Go into Politics?" in Cannon, James M., ed. *Politics USA.* Garden City, N.Y.: Doubleday, 1960, pp. 56–67. (Grass Roots Guide No. 4D).

"Time of Decision," *Vital Speeches,* July 15, 1960, pp. 580–83.

"The National Broadcasting Company Presents Senators John F. Kennedy, Lyndon B. Johnson, and Stuart Symington," *Meet the Press.* Washington, D.C.: Merkle Press. 35 pp.

"Acceptance Speech of Senator John F. Kennedy as Presidential Nominee to the Democratic National Convention," *Vital Speeches,* August 1, 1960, pp. 610–12.

"Candidates on Science: Kennedy Statement," *Science News Letter,* August 6, 1960, pp. 83 ff.

"We Must Climb to the Hilltop: A Discussion of National Purpose," *Life,* August 22, 1960, pp. 70–72.

"Book in the News: Review of B. H. Liddell Hart's *Deterrent or Defense,*" *Saturday Review,* September 3, 1960, pp. 17–18.

"A Day I'll Remember," *Look,* September 13, 1960, pp. 51–54 (re: Day following presidential nomination).

"Where the Candidates Stand: Interview," *Farm Journal,* October, 1960, pp. 36 ff.

"Special Report to Businessmen," *Executive,* October, 1960, pp. 3–5

"Q. and A.: The Hot Issues: Debate," *Newsweek,* October 3, 1960, pp. 42–44.

"If the Soviets Control Space—They Can Control Earth," *Missiles and Rockets,* October 10, 1960, pp. 12–13.

"The Role of the President" in *Representative American Speeches:* 1959–1969. New York: H. W. Wilson Co., 1960, pp. 123–130.

"As Kennedy Foresaw the Presidency: Although What Follows was Written in January, 1960, it Represents the Views of the President Elect Today," *U.S. News and World Report,* November 28, 1960, pp. 76–78.

The National Broadcasting Company Presents: Senator John F. Kennedy," *Meet the Press.* Washington, D.C.: Merkle Press, 1960. 14 pp.

"Kennedy Sizes up Kennedy: An Interview," *Newsweek,* March 21, 1960, pp. 39–40.

"Kennedy and Humphrey Answer Five Key Questions: An Interview," *New Leader,* March 28, 1960, pp. 3–7.

"Let's Get Rid of College Loyalty Oaths," *Coronet,* April, 1960, pp. 88–94.

"Should Congress Retain the Loyalty Provisions of the N.D.E.A.?" *Congressional Digest,* April 1960, pp. 111 ff.

"I am not the Catholic Candidate for President: Full Text of an

Address to the American Society of Newspaper Editors, April 21, 1960," *U.S. News and World Report,* May 2, 1960, pp. 90–92.

"What Senator Kennedy Says: An Interview on WRC-TV, May 14, 1960," *U.S. News and World Report,* June 13, 1960, pp. 122–23.

"Disarmament Can Be Won," *Bulletin of the Atomic Scientists,* June, 1960, pp. 217–19.

"Issue is Whether the Power of U.S. is Increasing," *U.S. News and World Report,* June 13, 1960, pp. 49–50. *Missiles and Rockets,* October 10, 1960, pp. 12–13.

"Kennedy on the Issues," *U.S. News and World Report,* October 10, 1960, pp. 84 ff.

"Nixon vs. Kennedy: Federal Aid to Education: Questions and Answers," *Senior Scholastic,* October 19, 1960, pp. 11 ff. Candidates and the Arts: A Letter to the Editor, *Saturday Review,* October 29, 1960, pp. 43–44.

"The Crisis in Foreign Affairs," *American Federationist,* November, 1960, pp. 7–11.

"An Interview with John Kennedy," *Bulletin of the Atomic Scientists,* November, 1960, pp. 346–47.

"New Frontiers: An Exclusive Interview," *Catholic World,* November, 1960, pp. 80–86.

"Kennedy Announces First Appointments, Discusses Election, Press Conference, November 19, 1960," *CQ Weekly Report,* November 19, 1960, pp. 1909–1913.

"President and President Elect Discuss Transfer of Executive Responsibility: Statement," *Department of State Bulletin,* December 26, 1960, p. 968.

1961

"John F. Kennedy on Libraries: Letter, August 19, 1960 to Minneapolis Public Library," *Wilson Library Bulletin,* January, 1961, p. 338.

Freedom of Communications: Final Report. U.S. Congress. Senate. Committee on Commerce, Subcommittee on Communications. Washington, D.C.: U.S. Government Printing Office. 1961. 2 vols. (1944, 699). (Speeches, debates, remarks, press conferences, and statements.)

"Kennedy Campaign Declarations listed—From His Acceptance Speech July 15, 1960, to the Eve of His Election November 7, 1960," *CQ Weekly Report,* January 13, 1961.

"How Does the President Feel About Counties?" *County Officer,* January, 1961, pp. 64.

"President Kennedy's Program: Texts of All the President's Messages to Congress, Major Statements, Speeches and Letters in the First 100 Days," Washington, D.C.: *Congressional Quarterly Service,* 1961, pp. 1–73.

"President-elect Kennedy Talks About Our Children," *Parents Magazine,* January, 1961, p. 35.

"We Can't Afford to Wait on Recreation," *Field and Stream,* January, 1961, p. 6.

"History will be our Judge: Address to the Massachusetts Legislature, January 9, 1961," *Vital Speeches,* February 1, 1960, pp. 227–28.

Inaugural Address Delivered at the Capitol, Washington, D.C., January 20, 1961. Washington, D.C.: U.S. Government Printing Office. 1961. ii, 3 pp. Also contained in *Public Papers,* 1961: No. 1.

"Kennedy's Own Words: How he Runs the White House Now: Excerpt from NBC Television Interview, April 11, 1961." *U.S. News and World Report,* April 24, 1961, p. 8.

"President Kennedy on International Educational Exchange," *School and Society,* Summer, 1961, p. 256.

"Message to you from the President," *Life,* September 15, 1961, p. 95.

"Every Citizen Holds Office: Excerpts from an Address Delivered in 1957," *NEA Journal,* October, 1961, pp. 18–20.

"Message from President Kennedy to National Foreign Trade Convention," *Department of State Bulletin,* November 20, 1961, p. 833.

1962

To Turn the Tide: A Selection from President Kennedy's Public Statements from his Election through the 1961 Adjournment of Congress, Setting forth the Goals of his First Legislative Year. Edited by John W. Gardner. Foreword by Carl Sandburg. Introduction by President Kennedy. New York: Harper & Row, 1962. 235 pp.

The Quotable Mr. Kennedy. Edited by Gerald C. Gardner. New York: Abelard-Schuman, 1962. 65 pp.

"The Arts in America," In *Creative America.* Washington, D.C.: Ridge Press. Published for the National Cultural Center, 1962, pp. 4–8.

"Next Twenty-Five Years," *Look,* January 16, 1962, p. 17.

"Exchange of Messages on the Question of Exploration of Outer Space," *United Nations Review,* April, 1962 (re: Exchange of Messages between Kennedy and Khrushchev).

"President Congratulates Venezuela on Firm Defense of Democracy: Letter, June 5, 1962," *Department of State Bulletin,* June 25, 1962, p. 1023.

"Vigor We Need," *Sports Illustrated,* July 16, 1962, pp. 12–14.

"Strength and Style of our Navy Tradition," *Life,* August 10, 1962, pp. 79 ff.

"President Kennedy to Prince Sihanouk: Letter August 31, 1962," *Department of State Bulletin,* September 24, 1962, pp. 456–57.

"Message," *Bulletin of the Atomic Scientists,* December, 1962, p. 2.

1963

Public Papers of the Presidents of the United States: Containing the Public Messages, Speeches, and Statements of the President, 1962. Washington, D.C.: U.S. Government Printing Office. 1963. 1019 pp. It should be noted that with rare exceptions material contained in the three annual volumes of Kennedy's *Public Papers* has not been separately listed in this complete listing of writing attributed to John F. Kennedy. The following citation is listed because it contains some items not found in *Public Papers.*

Presidential Documents published in the Federal Register During 1962. Supplement to Title 3, The President, Code of Federal Regulations. Published by the Office of the Federal Register. Washington, D.C.: U.S. Government Printing Office, 1963.

Public Papers of the Presidents of the United States, Containing the Public Messages, Speeches, and Statements of the President, January 2 to November 22, 1963. Washington, D.C.: U.S. Government Printing Office. 1964.

Private Letters of John F. Kennedy, Edited by R. G. Deindorfer, *Good Housekeeping,* February, 1963, pp. 74 ff.

"President Greets Conference of National Organizations; Letter, March 7, 1963, April 8, 1963, *Department of State Bulletin,* April 8, 1962, p. 531.

"President Cites Importance of Home Improvements Programs," *American Home,* April, 1963, p. 85.

"President's National Library Week Statement Stresses Education," *Publishers' Weekly,* April 22, 1962, p. 30.

Preventing Conflicts of Interest on the Part of Special Government Employees; The President's Memorandum of May 2, 1962. Washington, D.C.: U.S. Government Printing Office. 1963. 19 pp.

"Forward." In Sorensen, Theodore C., *Decision Making in the White House.* New York: Columbia University Press, 1963, pp. xi–xiv.

"Time the U.S. Caught Up; Excerpt from an Address to the National Council of Senior Citizens, June 13, 1963," *New Republic,* November 9, 1963, p. 35.

"President Kennedy Talks about You, Your Children and Peace," edited by Ray Robinson. *Good Housekeeping,* November 1963, pp. 73 ff.

"From the White House; Letter to the ALA Conference." *ALA Bulletin,* September, 1963, p. 733.

"What Business can do for America," *Nation's Business,* September 1963, pp. 29 ff.

"JFK: What Women can do Now for Peace: Interview," *McCall's,* November, 1963, pp. 102 ff.

1964

Public Papers of the Presidents of the United States, Containing the Public Messages, Speeches, and Statements of the President. January 2 to November 22, 1963. Washington, D.C.: U.S. Government Printing Office, 1964. 1,007 pp.

The Burden and the Glory: The Hopes and Purposes of President Kennedy's Second and Third Years in Office as Revealed in his Published Statements and Addresses. Edited by Allan Nevins. Foreword by President Lyndon B. Johnson. New York: Harper & Row, 1964. 293 pp.

A Nation of Immigrants. Introduction by Robert F. Kennedy. New York: Harper & Row, 1964, 160 pp. This is an expanded version of the 1958 pamphlet with the same title cited above.

CHAPTER II.

The Major Biographies*

Burns, James MacGregor. *John Kennedy: A Political Profile.* New York: Harcourt, Brace, 1960, 1961. 309 pp. Paperback ed., New York: Avon Books, 1961. 288 pp. The Avon edition contains an additional comment by Burns entitled "Inauguration 1961— A Foreword."

This is one of the dozen best biographies of an American political figure written in the twentieth century, and it is the best biography ever written about John F. Kennedy. Other biographies have the advantage of describing exciting Presidential actions of Kennedy, but it is Burns who tells us the most about what made the man tick and what elements were missing in that remarkable mixture which composed Kennedy's political character.

Burns has the advantage of telling a success story, whereas Sorensen and Schlesinger have to struggle to make interesting hundreds of pages of setbacks and frustrations: a giant America held at bay by a minor power off its Florida coast and being sucked deeper and deeper into a galling and unpopular war on the mainland of Asia; an imaginative

---

* Material from these major biographies is, of course, crucial to study relating to most of the other categories of this bibliography.

domestic program bottled up in Congress; and a proposed detente with Russia that never fully developed. It may well be that the chronicles of Kennedy's Presidency made this period look more heroic and more interesting than Burns would have; nevertheless, Burns' book honestly prepares us for the frustrations that were to come.

This political profile establishes beyond serious question that Senator John Kennedy was far more genuinely intelligent, thoughtful, and politically able than his critics and some of his friends believed. Although Burns is the only biographer who doesn't make Kennedy look larger than life (even critic Victor Lasky makes Kennedy out as unbelievably steeped in fraud and mischief), he does emerge from Burns' searching biography more impressive than one would have expected. At the same time, Burns' book is well documented, and in a fair-minded way prepares us not to expect Kennedy's meteoric career to come to full fruition—assassination or not.

The Kennedy revealed in Burns' book is as attractive as Schlesinger's Kennedy because the portrait is complete—the brashness, the burning ambition, the deviousness are all there as Burns throws relentless light into the innermost recesses of Kennedy's life. In Burns' book, too, just as in an article he was later to write for the *New York Times Magazine* in 1962 (entry #82), the biographer criticizes Kennedy for a lack of heartfelt commitment to progressive legislation—a commitment which was necessary if Kennedy was to rally solid support for his goals. Furthermore, Burns faces squarely the connections between the personal qualities and mental traits of Kennedy the man and the response of Kennedy the office holder to such specific public questions as McCarthyism, civil rights, and Catholicism. Only Richard Whalen in *The Founding Father* (entry #30) is more unsparing, while remaining responsible.

Yet Burns reveals so much else about Kennedy—his openminded inquiry, his wry self-examination, the steady growth in vision, a genuine devotion to the public welfare, and, above all, a firm fiber of integrity bridging Kennedy's occasional lapses of judgment—that there emerges a winning portrait of the most promising and exciting person to enter the White House in more than a quarter century.

In addition to the integrity and great skill of Burns as a political analyst and biographer, the quality of this book springs from the circumstances of its writing. Burns, a Williams College, Massachusetts, political scientist and biographer of Franklin D. Roosevelt, wanted to determine for himself what kind of a President Kennedy might make before deciding whether to accept Kennedy's offer of a substantial job on his Senate staff. His literary and interview research on this subject led to a biography and mutual friendship and respect, but not to a job. Burns' independence of judgment, as this book and subsequent annotated articles testify, was never impaired by his being an insider nor was he ever overwhelmed by the personality of a man imbued with tremendous charm and power. While not a complete insider, Burns had "complete and unrestricted access to his [Kennedy's] personal and official files" which was never granted anyone else and which few promising politicians would grant anyone with Burns' perception.

The chapter and source notes are superb and should continue indefinitely to be used by researchers as they have been in the past. Thus, Kennedy's early years and political and intellectual growth, as well as the political background of his legislative and campaign decisions, are set out with unexcelled authority and detail.

Burns is a reformist, liberal political scientist who puts great store in matching action with ideals; that this is an extremely difficult task is well known by Burns, who himself has run for public office. He avoids imposing his ideals when evaluating Kennedy, but instead, he scrupulously attempts to measure Kennedy by Kennedy's own political standards.

The book has a pleasant, straightforward style, but the author's graceful writing never intrudes on the story being told. (See also "Kennedy and his Biographers" in the "Introductory Essay.")

Sorensen, Theodore C. *Kennedy.* New York: Harper & Row, 1965. 783 pp.

This is the most important book for readers interested in the facts of the Kennedy Presidency, and a very important one for readers interested in Kennedy the man. "This book does not purport to be a full-scale biography of John Kennedy or a comprehensive history of this era," says Sorensen. "Yet it is more than a personal memoir." Indeed it has more firsthand and significant information than any of the other contributions to the Kennedy Literature. All serious research about what happened in the Kennedy Administration must begin and center around the material in this book.

Sorensen's book is offered as a substitute for the memoirs Kennedy would have written (or more exactly, Kennedy would have written with the assistance of Sorensen). In many ways Sorensen is the ideal man to undertake this task, being at Kennedy's side perhaps more than any other person when the important decisions were made and when significant developments occurred. There was also, says Sorensen, "a bond of intimacy in which there were few secrets and no illusions."

Sorensen, who met the subject of his book when Kennedy was a Senator, opens with a discussion of "The Emerging Kennedy" in which he treats him as an individual, a Senator, and a politician. He describes "The Kennedy Candidacy" in the second section and "The Kennedy Presidency" in the third. The fourth section deals with "President Kennedy and the Nation"; the fifth, with "President Kennedy and the World."

Kennedy's book would have come largely from the same files and memoranda and letters as did Sorensen's—there is no evidence that either of them kept a systematic diary or journal containing their observation of events and personalities as they appeared to them at the moment.

It is possible to speculate on what type of book Kennedy would have written. The late President would not have felt, in all probability, as much need to make deletions for security reasons. Neither would he have felt his friend's remorseless need to refute each petty detractor.

For all that, this is a very fine book. In addition to using his own files, Sorensen has cross-checked with the major magazine files and has made use of the scrapbooks of others as a memory check. He properly admits to being a strong partisan of President Kennedy but within that relationship he maintains high standards of judgment.

The main aim of Sorensen's book—to make a case for Kennedy as a doer and achiever—is, for many readers, only partially achieved. While it will not win over all doubters, the case should be examined carefully before one accepts the glib generalization that Kennedy was all style with nothing to show for it. Sorensen is most convincing when he shows us how many projects—the Peace Corps, Anti-Poverty Program, Nuclear Test Ban Treaty, Civil Rights Act, Trade Expansion Act, Mental Health and Mental Retardation Acts, Higher Education and Medical Education Acts, Manpower Development and Retraining Act, the commitment to the development of outer space, the modernization of the New Deal-Fair Deal measures, Twenty-fourth

Amendment (outlawing poll tax), Community Health Facilities Act, Communications Satellite Act and Educational Television Act — were initiated or carried out by Kennedy during his Presidency. And there is much merit to Sorensen's claim that, despite difficulties, many more programs would have been achieved before Kennedy left office.

Schlesinger, Arthur, Jr. *A Thousand Days: John F. Kennedy in the White House.* Boston: Houghton Mifflin Company, 1965. 1087 pp.

This book ranks alongside the Burns and Sorensen volumes as an indispensable biography of Kennedy the political man. It is outranked only by Sorensen's book as a record of what occurred during Kennedy's occupancy of the White House. It penetrates much deeper than any of the other books into the implications and consequences of plans and actions undertaken by the government during the Kennedy years, particularly in foreign affairs. (The Burns biography, of course, does not extend beyond the inauguration of Kennedy.) This brilliant historian's immense knowledge of public affairs here and abroad and his familiarity with public figures and the world of ideas as well as his dogged determination to educate his reader permit him to sketch in background material in a meaningful way not found elsewhere. The book's true merit, and not just the "best seller" qualities, won for it the Pulitzer Prize for Biography and the National Book Award.

Schlesinger has the advantage of working from a journal which he kept after his first weeks in the White House and his quotations carry the authenticity of having come from almost immediate notation rather than from memory. Like Sorensen, he acknowledges there are sometimes more than one version of a given occurrence and when this happens, the author simply has to use his judgment about which one to use. A footnoted manuscript of this book will be available "at an appropriate time" at the Kennedy Library, where it is now deposited along with Schlesinger's own White House files.

Schlesinger is extraordinarily good on sketching in personalities because he is an imaginative historian who finds individuals engaging and who knows of their importance in affecting events. (An exception is the rather sketchy portrait of McGeorge Bundy whom Schlesinger acknowledges was as important a man as Sorensen on policy questions facing Kennedy during his early months in the White House.) Many of the persons Schlesinger likes or admires, he admits others saw as arrogant, ruthless, or abrasive. He concentrates unduly on his friends and acquaintances from Harvard and M.I.T. and even speaks of the "Charles River doctrine" on a given question. A great amount of space is given to John Kenneth Galbraith because he is a friend, and to Adlai Stevenson because of old and affectionate associations rather than because of Stevenson's official relationship with Kennedy.

Generally Schlesinger is surprisingly kind to most of the figures who strut across the Kennedy stage, but the White House historian is a strong partisan when it comes to the unceasing battle between the White House staff and the bureaucracy. A considerable controversy has arisen over allegedly unseemly belittling of Secretary of State Dean Rusk, an easy target, but a hard man to knock over. A rereading of Schlesinger does not leave the impression that Rusk was given less than his due. The problem seems to have been that both Rusk and Schlesinger kept on being what they had been before—Rusk an Assistant Secretary and Foundation bureaucrat and Schlesinger a liberal professor and paper grader (in this case penciling caustic comments on State Department reports).

In the late spring of 1962 Kennedy drove around Cambridge and selected a site for the library which would house the President's papers and become a center of research on the Presidency. In October of 1963, while completing the documents for acquiring the necessary land from Harvard University, Kennedy had Schlesinger reword some phrases about transferring the land whenever the President requested it. Who knows, Kennedy remarked, who will be President next year.

Schlesinger's footnoted manuscript to this text, when it becomes available at an appropriate time, will make a splendid contribution to research at the Kennedy Library. But a greater contribution to those interested in Kennedy is this library without walls, *A Thousand Days.*

Lincoln, Evelyn. *My Twelve Years with John F. Kennedy.* New York: David McKay, Inc., 1965. Paperback ed., New York: Bantam, 1966. 311 pp.

Samuel Johnson maintained that biography reached the average reader more quickly than history, because the similarities of all men permit an average reader to identify himself with anyone about whom he reads. This is not quite true; Kennedy was a person in background and qualities so different from the norm that many readers can best approach him through the connecting link of an author who has sprung much more from the rib of America. In this case, the author is Mrs. Evelyn Lincoln, whose book *My Twelve Years with John F. Kennedy* describes her eventful career—daughter of a Nebraska congressman, college drama student, and member of a husband and wife team who, like Kennedy, passionately believed that politics, despite its familiar seaminess, was the most exciting, constructive, and noble profession in which one could engage.

Endowed with shrewd foresight, Mrs. Lincoln had picked Kennedy out in 1952 as the man who would become the next Democratic President (to her, Republican Presidents didn't really count), and as his personal secretary she reacts to the great people and events of the period.

When a resounding voice announced her at the Elysée Palace as "Madame Lincoln," the President, dressed in white tie and tails, standing next to General De Gaulle in full dress uniform, "began to laugh when he heard my introduction, and I was so amused I hardly knew what I said to General De Gaulle when I shook his hand."

No other biography on the maturing Kennedy does more to show the young millionaire gallant—courting, campaigning, marrying, teasing, getting angry, maneuvering with and without crutches, sauntering on and off airplanes, and sailing boats, and all the while knitting together the team and public image which would eventually send him to the White House.

Mrs. Lincoln disclaims giving political analysis, but she is a useful cross-check on what others say; she is perhaps the most constant link between various personalities and events Kennedy was to confront after 1953, but she was no political innocent. When she received frantic calls from bureaucratic officials objecting to her having Kennedy's messages to Cabinet members and other officials hand-delivered rather than sent through regular channels, Mrs. Lincoln replied that that was what the President wanted. "He wanted action, and he had found this was the way he could get it."

Mrs. Lincoln is well aware that Kennedy was essentially a political man; on his wedding night at New York City's Waldorf Astoria hotel, he rushed off a note to his secretary about a forthcoming speaking engagement.

82 THE KENNEDY LITERATURE

Her record comes primarily from a well-kept diary and other written records, as well as from remembrances of herself and her husband, Mr. Harold "Abe" Lincoln, who is a trained political scientist as well as politician. The book's virtue is that it achieved Mrs. Lincoln's steadily interesting style and, that unlike some other biographies, it benefits from neither the additions nor deletions suggested by members of the President's immediate family. The book's essential accuracy seems beyond doubt.

My Twelve Years leaves no doubt of the cruel distortion which political life brings to the family life of anyone who succumbs to its lure, but Mrs. Lincoln tells us how much the President was able to keep love and beauty in his family life.

During his Maryland Presidential primary, Kennedy spoke to me about the reliability and resourcefulness of Evelyn Lincoln. His faith was well-founded.

CHAPTER III.

Personal Material, Including Kennedy's Growth, Family, and His Circle

Hersey, John, "Survival," *The New Yorker,* June 17, 1944, pp. 31 ff.
    This was the first account of Kennedy's South Pacific exploit, later reprinted in the *Reader's Digest.* A brief version of it was widely distributed in Kennedy's first race for Congress.

Healy, Paul F., "The Senate's Gay Young Bachelor," *Saturday Evening Post,* June 13, 1953, pp. 25 ff.
    The use Kennedy made of his youthful personality is perhaps best illustrated in this piece. Rather than being embarrassed by his youthful vigor, the Senator seemed to thrive on it. Richard Whalen, in *The Founding Father,* states that shortly before the article was published, the future Mrs. Jacqueline Kennedy telephoned her aunt to ask her not to make public her engagement to the Senator or else the magazine would scrap the piece.

Dinneen, Joseph. *The Kennedy Family.* Boston: Little Brown, 1959. 238 pp.
    This is a Boston reporter's view of the family after following Joseph Kennedy and his family for twenty years, but with many of the anec-

dotes left out which reporters found worth talking about over a beer. One of the items which was deleted from Dinneen's newspaper version of the book because of a stern phone call from John F. Kennedy (then a nervous candidate for President), was an interesting interview by Dinneen with Joe Kennedy regarding anti-semitism. This interview appears in Whalen's *The Founding Father*, pp. 278–380.

Donovan, Robert J. *PT 109: John F. Kennedy in World War II.* New York: McGraw-Hill, 1961. 247 pp. Paperback ed., New York: Crest, 1962. 160 pp.

In re-creating Kennedy's heroic wartime experiences, this Washington political writer interviewed members of the crew of Lt. John Kennedy's ill-fated PT boat and visited the Pacific Island near which the Japanese destroyer sliced the boat in half. It is a splendid children's story, but adults will also find in it an authentic record of the young Kennedy's courage and resourcefulness when the chips were down. His warm sense of camaraderie and his concern for his fellow men in this episode are established beyond doubt. Kennedy took pride in giving advice about the filming of the movie version of this story, but he seldom spoke of the exploit and passed off the opportunity of using it on a television show with the terse remark that it was "an interesting experience." When a young lad during the Wisconsin campaign asked Kennedy how he became a war hero, Kennedy shot back: "It was easy. They sunk my boat." In a letter to Donovan, President Kennedy attested to the accuracy of Donovan's account.

Lowe, Jacques. *Portrait: The Emergence of John F. Kennedy.* New York: McGraw-Hill, 1961. 223 pp.

While also valuable for sentimental reasons, this is the most useful of the photo books recalling to life the political man Kennedy was. It covers his childhood, Congressional period, social life, and campaigns, with some revealing photos seldom seen elsewhere.

Collins, Frederic W., "The Mind of John F. Kennedy," *New Republic,* May 8, 1961, pp. 15–20.

This is probably the worst serious piece ever written about Kennedy. It describes Kennedy as the star quarterback of the Administration who chomps up data, plants ideas in Louis Mountbatten's mind, fires off questions, plows his way through bureaucratic undergrowth, and dazzles everyone, especially Washington correspondent Collins, with his mastery of detailed knowledge and his "solo performance as decider." Undaunted by the fact that between the writing and publication of this piece the Bay of Pigs fiasco exposed how shallow all this razzle-dazzle could be, Collins in a footnote insists that the Cuban experience only confirms the excellence of Kennedy's hyperactivities, and the author urges him to continue in the same manner, for "the carryover of preordained alternatives will dwindle with some speed." Of course these "carry-overs" never did; it is revealing that in this article, as in a considerable portion of the Kennedy literature, the Kennedy "mind" is defined solely in terms of technique, as if values, heart, and commitment were irrelevant.

Holcombe, Arthur, "John F. Kennedy '40 as Presidential Cabinet Maker," *Harvard Alumni Bulletin,* May 27, 1961.

One of Kennedy's college professors recalls Kennedy as a student of political science and comments upon his political maturation and judgment.

"The Richest President, How Much He Has, How Much He Gets," *U.S. News & World Report,* January 18, 1962, pp. 82 ff.

This is one of the few articles to attempt specific estimates of how wealthy John Kennedy was. Since the Kennedys kept the information on the extent of their wealth private, this article can only be used as speculation. *U.S. News* kept up a running barrage against Kennedy throughout his Presidency, particularly on the subject of Cuba. Sorensen records that Kennedy almost never read the magazine "on the ground that it had little news and less to report." In this particular instance, though, *U.S. News* reported Kennedy was worth several millions of dollars. Burns also makes some estimates on the Kennedy wealth and campaign expenditures, but they are somewhat sketchy. The President gave his salary while in office to charity, and, after selling television rights to *Profiles in Courage,* he was reported to have turned over to charity $350,000 in royalties from that book's earnings.

"Kennedy and his Confessional," *Time*, March 16, 1962, p. 73.

One of the few articles that goes right to the technical question which was of concern to unbigoted non-Catholics. According to church law, all Catholics must go to confession at least once a year. A President may choose his own confessor whose identity is unlikely to be disclosed. Could a confessor advise a Catholic President that a given policy of his was contrary to church doctrine? The answer is negative, according to this article which quotes a speech on the subject by Father John L. Reedy, editor of the Catholic weekly *Ave Maria*. Father Reedy explains that the confessor does not give technical advice and that the responsibility for policy decision rests with the President alone. Father Reedy also remarks that "a few of the religious spokesmen who voiced pre-election fears have unfairly implied that Mr. Kennedy is a good Catholic President because he is a bad Catholic."

"Kennedy Marriage Rumor Out in the Open," *Editor and Publisher*, September 22, 1962, p. 107.

In March, 1962, an irreverent New York monthly, *The Realist*, published an account of an alleged earlier marriage of John F. Kennedy. The claim then travelled underground until it reached a Capitol Hill magazine, *Roll Call*, which on August 23, 1962, printed: "The newshawks are working overtime to confirm a report on an alleged prior marriage of a high government official. So far, they've drawn only blanks."

At this point, Kennedy felt that the allegation had to be answered. *Newsweek* Magazine and the *Washington Post*, two publications owned by Kennedy's friend and supporter Philip Graham, carried denials of the rumor. The rumor had been based upon the Blauvelt family genealogy, said the publications, the accuracy of which was challenged by a White House spokesman. Press Secretary Pierre Salinger limited his comment to the terse statement: "The President's wife is his first and only one." Kennedy himself refused all public comment, but Sorensen reports the President was more angered by this rumor than by any of the many others which surrounded his life.

The *New York Times*, on September 18 and 20, 1962, researched the story in a serious way, giving summations of one critic who believed that the Blauvelt family genealogy had some merit and many more who did not. The *Times* concluded that the rumor was unfounded.

The *Editor and Publisher article,* which uses the first person singular, but oddly enough is unsigned, examines the impact of the rumor; it notes that *Parade Magazine* received 12,000 letters of inquiry about it; the American right wing used it; and it made front page headlines in Britain. The article also examines the ethical difficulties the press faces in deciding how and whether to treat such rumors and quotes the editor of the *New York World Telegram and Sun* in support of their position: "Printing rumors is not good journalism. Some readers will be left with a lingering misapprehension, even though you state that the story is untrue." This is, of course, a real risk, but political scientists, historians, and biographers must nevertheless be concerned about the impact of rumor on the capacity of a political figure to govern.

Manchester, William. *Portrait of a President: John F. Kennedy in Profile.* Boston: Little, Brown and Company, 1962. 238 pp. Paperback ed., New York: MacFadden-Bartell, 1964. 158 pp.

Manchester, a Washington journalist, has spun out into book form about three basic interviews (and a score of minor ones) and most of the engaging anecdotes readily available in Washington at the time the book was written in 1962. *Portrait of a President* is entertaining and unpretentious journalism, told with a swift style that *Teens* Magazine called "immensely readable." Of special interest is the "Author's Note" at the beginning, revealing with great frankness how such a book is created. During Manchester's interview with Kennedy, the President seemed to have been preoccupied with other matters, as his drumming fingers should have warned the author, but his interview with Arthur Krock, the cagey Kennedy family friend was more successful, and provides us with new information and viewpoints. The author's interview with the President's father, something not easily come by, is both touching and revealing. Joseph Kennedy said of his son in the White House:

> I know nothing can happen to him. I tell you something's watching out for him. I've stood by his deathbed four times. Each time I said good-by to him he always came back . . . When you've

been through something like that back, and the Pacific, what can hurt you? Who's going to scare you?

The book is descriptive and uncritical, the author stating: "I revere the Presidency and admire this President." Manchester was authorized by the President's widow to write a detailed history of Kennedy's assassination in Dallas.

Sidey, Hugh. *John F. Kennedy, President.* **New York: Atheneum, 1963. 400 pp. Revised Edition, New York: Atheneum, 1964. 434 pp.**

Although this work has been surpassed in depth of analysis and extent of new information by the major Presidential biographies of Sorensen and Schlesinger, those who wish a fast-paced, fair-minded journalistic coverage of most of the major events of the Kennedy tenure, by one who saw the President often but who was not officially responsible to him, will find this descriptive narrative of interest. Sidey, a fourth-generation journalist trained in the Middle West, covered John Kennedy in Washington for *Time* Magazine since 1958. Even for serious journalism, however, the book lacks depth and stubbornly refuses to ask what the events described mean.

Shaw, Mark. *The John F. Kennedys, A Family Album.* **New York: Farrar, Strauss, 1964. 159 pp.**

These are the photos favored greatly by Mrs. Jacqueline Kennedy. They stress the happy times of the Kennedy's lives, and create a rather romantic aura.

Sargent, H. and others, "Versailles on the Potomac: A Report to the Bourgeoisie," *Esquire* **Magazine, January, 1963. pp. 41–47.**

A satire on what some critics believed to be the royal tone that White House entertainment had taken on under the Kennedys.

Heller, Deane and David. *Jacqueline Kennedy.* **Paperback, Derby, Connecticut: Monarch Books, Inc., 1963. New enlarged edition. 222 pp.**

There is no very satisfactory biography of Mrs. John F. Kennedy. The most literate piece about her, but not a biography, is Katherine

Anne Porter's "Her Legend Will Live," carried in the *Ladies Home Journal.* Her significance for Kennedy's public emerges adequately in the books by Sorensen, Schlesinger, and Evelyn Lincoln. This book by the Heller writing team combs through the available public anecdotes about Mrs. Kennedy before and after her marriage. Her role in the 1960 campaign is interestingly told. Adjectives like "magnificent" are used indiscriminately but on the whole the book is factual and descriptive rather than gushy. In considering the impact of the Kennedy literature, this book is important if for no other reason than it had sold over 2,000,000 copies before it was rushed back into print in December, 1963, with some additional material.

Whalen, Richard J. *The Founding Father: The Story of Joseph P. Kennedy and the Family He Raised to Power.* Paperback, New York: New American Library, 1964. 532 pp.

This biography is built up from "Mr. Kennedy, the Chairman," an unsigned article on Joseph P. Kennedy written by Robert Cantwell of Time, Inc., which appeared in *Fortune* Magazine (Sept. 1937), and which for 25 years was the standard work on a financier who was almost as enigmatic as Howard Hughes. Much of the data of Joseph Kennedy's life is unrecorded, which made author Whalen rely upon extensive interviews with reliable informants. Not surprisingly, Joseph Kennedy refused him an interview and other cooperation, but the friends and some of the business and political associates of the "Founding Father" were more cooperative. Arthur Krock of *The New York Times,* who had a long and friendly association with Joseph Kennedy as well as with his family, gave Whalen access to some of his unpublished manuscript material, revealing a documentary source of importance to Kennedy research which will later become accessible to scholars.

Whalen uses his interviews judiciously and the testimony seems to ring true, although there are secondary source materials which sometimes seem less reliable. Whalen, a writer for *Fortune,* has had the advantage of critical textual advice from editors of that magazine, which is a repository of realistic knowledge about the connections between business and politics. The biography is happily undistorted by any excessive focusing upon the relationship between the father and his most renowned son, and what is revealed largely confirms Joseph

Kennedy's influence on President Kennedy's policy matters as remarkably slight. During the entire Kennedy Administration, however, there are persistent suggestions that Joseph Kennedy may have had decisive influence at times on Presidential appointments and nominations, and neither Whalen nor the biographers of John Kennedy are able either to confirm this or to convince us that we should dismiss this possibility.

Whalen's description of Joseph Kennedy's open-handed use of his enormous wealth, powerful business connections, and influence on his sons' behalf is an instructive lesson to those people who think that all it took for John Kennedy to get to the top was intelligence, energy, charm, shrewd political judgment, and dedication to public service. Of all the writers discussed in this critical bibliography, the very perceptive Whalen is one of the least dazzled by any of the Kennedys.

Lowe, Jacques. *The Kennedy Years.* Text prepared by *The New York Times* under the direction of Harold Faber. New York: Viking, 1964. 327 pp.

From one of the richest collections of Kennedy photos (Lowe has taken about 30,000), the photographer has selected some three hundred which cover most aspects of Kennedy's personal and political life. The book includes some photographs taken by George Tames, a *New York Times* Washington photographer. The text is most helpful in making clear either what the pictures represent or the circumstances under which they were taken, although other books which concentrate on fewer aspects of Kennedy years will obviously be more detailed as to subject matter. Also see previous Lowe work cited in this section of bibliography.

Settle, Trudy S. (ed.). *The Faith of John F. Kennedy.* Introduction by Richard Cardinal Cushing. New York: Dutton, 1965. 127 pp.

This work contains many excerpts from Kennedy's speeches dealing with or touching upon faith or religious matters; it also contains biblical extracts used as sources for his speeches. Settle offers little textual explanation other than date and place of speeches. Cardinal Cushing, a religious leader who was a close friend of Kennedy, testified that he was a man of strong religious conviction. Although his religion was more talked about than any other President's, the Cardinal notes,

"President Kennedy wore his religion, like his patriotism, lightly, and, again like his patriotism, he felt his religion profoundly." Except for the Cardinal's Introduction, those who take the book's title seriously will be disappointed, although readers merely interested in the sources of Kennedy's biblical quotations and allusions in Kennedy's writings and speeches will be satisfied.

Timmisch, Nick and Johnson, William. *Robert Kennedy at 40.* **New York: W. W. Norton and Company, 1965. 304 pp.**

Most of the books on Robert Kennedy have been thin, both in substance and bulk. Here, two *Time* writers set forth the main facts of Robert Kennedy's adult life in a reasonably objective way. Until the Robert Kennedy literature is important in itself, readers of the John Kennedy literature will be more interested in Timmisch's and Johnson's sections dealing with Robert's relations with his brother John, for whom he served as Attorney General, and his position as the eldest surviving son. The discussion of his senatorial campaign in New York does much to answer the question of whether the Joe Jr.—John —Robert—Edward Kennedy tradition will be continued.

Salinger, Pierre. *With Kennedy.* **New York: Doubleday and Co., 1966. 391 pp.**

The man who was press secretary to Kennedy from 1959 to 1963 does not add much to the picture of Kennedy which others have already given, but the book does give interesting firsthand evidence of Kennedy's talented use of public relations. Salinger's views of his own and Kennedy's various encounters with the Soviets are also of interest. It should be noted that Salinger was not a party to the major decisions of state, but instead was later informed of these decisions, which he subsequently had to explain to the public. Salinger remains a strong partisan of the Kennedy Administration and seems ready to join should there be another.

Fay, Paul B., Jr. *The Pleasure of His Company.* **New York: Harper & Row, Publishers, 1966. 262 pp.**

A friend of the President from PT boat days, Fay had participated in Kennedy's first Boston campaign, at which time he had prophesied correctly that he would one day become Kennedy's Under Secretary of the Navy. Kennedy kept his social life largely separate from his working life. (Sorensen, for example, participated little more than Sherman Adams did in Eisenhower's social life.) Fay, an amusing and easygoing fellow, takes the reader (who wishes to go) into those areas of the President's periods of relaxation and pleasure and his good-natured, "old buddy" joshing. Unfortunately, most of the humor doesn't come off. The White House was not a good place for making new friends and he thought he'd keep his old ones, Kennedy said when entering the Presidency. Fay was one of those old friends, but no other qualifying factors seem to have entitled him to write a book about his friendship with Kennedy.

CHAPTER IV.

Campaigns

"A Kennedy Runs for Congress: The Boston-Bred Scion of a former Ambassador Is a Fighting-Irish Conservative." *Look,* June 11, 1946, pp. 32 ff.

Stresses war record and family background of young candidate and Navy Veteran John F. Kennedy. Kennedy did not stress issues in his first campaign, but the magazine assumed he would follow in father's footsteps, especially in foreign policy questions. *Look* later became a major vehicle for Kennedy material, much of it quite helpful to his career. This early period of Kennedy's career is best described in James M. Burns' biography of Kennedy. Also see for patriotic aspect of the campaign "Promise Kept," *Time,* July 1, 1946, p. 23.

Vanocur, Sander, "Humphrey v. Kennedy; High Stakes in Wisconsin," *Reporter,* March 17, 1960, pp. 28–30.

A good description of the Kennedy gamble in Wisconsin, why he entered supposedly "Humphrey" territory, and Kennedy's lack of regular Democratic leadership support.

Chamberlain, John, "The Chameleon Image of John F. Kennedy," *National Review,* April 23, 1960, pp. 41–50.

A conservative writer in this lively conservative publication develops what he contends are conflicting positions Kennedy had taken on various domestic and foreign issues—particularly stressing economic issues. Kennedy had to make a concerted effort to answer such charges, which risked alienating liberals as well as conservatives.

Blagden, Ralph M., "Cabot Lodge's Toughest Fight," *Reporter,* September, 1952, pp. 10–11.

This piece is a journalist's description of the problems of one politician descended from an established Massachusetts family, Henry Cabot Lodge, facing the scion of an emerging family of power, John Kennedy.

Phillips, Cabell, "Case History of a Senate Race," *New York Times Magazine,* October 26, 1952, pp. 10 ff.

One of the most evocative and serious portraitists of political campaigns describes the Kennedy tea parties during elections and the work of John Kennedy's mother, Rose Kennedy, and the rest of the family in Kennedy's race against Senator Henry Cabot Lodge.

"Can the Catholic Vote Swing an Election?" *U. S. News & World Report,* August 10, 1956, pp. 41–46.

This is the complete version of the so-called Bailey Memorandum which Sorensen prepared at Kennedy's request, but which Sorensen denied drafting. Instead, he attributed it in general to "backers of Senator Kennedy," and specifically to campaign stalwart John Bailey. The Memorandum contained election district analyses, polls, quotes, and arguments designed to prove that Adlai Stevenson was weak among Catholic voters and would need a Catholic Vice Presidential running mate to win. Sorensen admits that the Memorandum, aimed at laymen, "oversimplified, overgeneralized and overextended premises in order to reach an impressive conclusion." Sorensen claims the deception was justifiable because it helped counter a prejudicial argument circulating which maintained that a Catholic on the ticket would cost the Democrats votes. Critics argue, however, that Kennedy backers were ruthlessly threatening that Catholics would stay away from the Democratic party unless they were allowed a Catholic on the ticket. The next week, *U.S. News* ran a statistical piece entitled "More

About the 'Catholic Vote' in U.S. Elections," compiled largely by pollster Louis Bean, which argued that the Republicans had not, in fact, made spectacular gains among Catholic voters in recent years. In reviewing the Bailey Memorandum, it appears true that Kennedy took the lead in projecting the "Catholic Issue" publicly into the center of Democratic politics in the late 1950's. It is also true that the Catholic issue was always there beneath the surface and would have to come to the top later on, anyway.

Osborne, John, "The Economics of the Candidates," *Fortune*, October, 1960, pp. 136 ff.

This reporter on economics and public affairs gives a careful and generally objective analysis of what could be reasonably expected of the two candidates judging from their statements, records, commitments, advisors, and observed attitudes. While Nixon is found to be a "modern Republican" in outlook, Kennedy is much more inclined toward welfare state and pro-union measures.

Turnbull, John W., "The Clergy Faces Mr. Kennedy," *Reporter*, October 23, 1960, pp. 32–34.

A vivid description of candidate Kennedy skillfully turning to his own advantage the critical questions of Protestant ministers he met at the Greater Houston Ministerial Association, Houston, Texas, September 12, 1960.

Wicklin, John, "Protestant and Catholic Votes Found to Offset Each Other in Kennedy's Victory," *New York Times*, November 11, 1960, p. 23.

This *New York Times* roundup of reports from political leaders and correspondents around the country showed the Republican leaders did not believe their Catholic vote had fallen off as much as was feared, while Democratic leaders claimed that conservative Protestants outside the South came out strongly against Kennedy. The newspaper noted, too, that the religious issue seemed to affect only certain areas of the nation. While a "strong, silent 'Protestant vote' cut into Senator John F. Kennedy's margin of victory . . . this was more than offset by a more strategically placed 'Catholic vote' which aided the Senator in large states where he needed to win." Elmo Roper, in "Polling Post-

Mortem" (*Saturday Review,* November 26, 1960), indicated a 62 per cent nationwide shift of Eisenhower Catholic voters to Kennedy. (The *Tribune's* poll analysis of Protestant voters was carried the next day.) A useful, if cautious, review of this sticky question may be found in Angus Campbell *et al., The American Voter* (abridged), New York: John Wiley and Sons, Inc., 1964.

Perhaps the wisest comment on the problem was made by Kennedy's father, Joseph Kennedy, who remarked: "I thought he would get a bigger Catholic vote than he did . . . [and] I did not think so many would vote against him because of his religion." Many of the Kennedy political strategists concur.

Knebel, Fletcher, "Pulitzer Prize Entry: John F. Kennedy," in *Candidates 1960.* Edited by Eric Sevareid. New York: Basic Books, 1959, pp. 181-215.

The colorful veteran reporter captures some of the stronger flavor of Kennedy's Boston campaigns for Congress and the Senate and of Massachusetts politics in general.

Schlesinger, Arthur M., Jr. *Kennedy or Nixon; Does It Make Any Difference?* New York: Macmillan, 1960. 51 pp.

Allowing for hindsight, it is surprising that a book with such a title had to be written, but the fact that both Kennedy and Schlesinger thought it had to be is in itself revealing. Schlesinger, after having annihilated Nixon for the benefit of liberal intellectuals, then undertakes the more difficult task of justifying to those same liberals the apparent Kennedy lapses in commitment to liberty which Burns had mercilessly exposed in his biography of the Presidential candidate.

In words which might well have either embarrassed or amused Kennedy, Schlesinger wrote: "Once Kennedy resolved the problem of his own identity, his own emotions were liberated for an increasingly forceful commitment to liberalism."

Of course, Kennedy knew that writers and readers of books needed such assurances much more than the average voters. Victor Lasky maintains that Schlesinger's work so enraged him that he sat down to write in two weeks *John F. Kennedy: What's Behind the Image?"*

White, Theodore. *The Making of the President, 1960.* New York: Atheneum, 1961, 400 pp. Paperback ed., New York: Pocketbooks, 1965. 481 pp.

This is an extremely detailed and at times exciting description of all the important incidents in the political campaigns of Kennedy and Nixon, written by an excellent reporter who traveled with both candidates during the election. White perceptively interviewed most of the important people on both sides in the campaign (with the notable exception of Nixon, who declined to give him an interview) and analyzes the relevant information. The book does more than much other reportage to help the reader understand Nixon as well as Kennedy, but at the end the reader tends to wonder why Kennedy didn't win by a landslide and why almost half the electorate chose Nixon. The political apparatus of these two men and the different group reactions to their appearances are more clearly and interestingly presented here than in any other book.

Much of the press had been reserved toward Kennedy during his struggle for nomination, but once Nixon became his opponent, many of the journalists actively supported Kennedy. White tells how

> when the bus or plane rolled or flew through the night [the journalists] sang songs of their own composition about Mr. Nixon and the Republicans in chorus with the Kennedy staff and felt that they, too, were marching like soldiers of the Lord to the New Frontiers.

Nixon's complaints on this score were not without merit.

Ironically, former Senator Barry Goldwater told a correspondent (*New York Times Magazine,* June 19, 1966, p. 52):

> My nomination resulted from our carefully reading *The Making of the President* and other books about Jack Kennedy's campaign. We ran a campaign like Jack ran a campaign. Now he was lauded to heaven—brilliant strategist, this, that and the other thing. We've been called Hitlers, Mussolinis and the convention has been called a *Putsch.* . . .

The Speeches, Remarks and Press Conferences of Senator John F. Kennedy and Vice President Richard M. Nixon. U.S.

98 THE KENNEDY LITERATURE

Congress, Senate Subcommittee on Communications of the Committee on Commerce, Report 994, 87th Congress, 1st Session. Part I: The Campaign Speeches of John F. Kennedy; Part II: The Campaign Speeches of Richard M. Nixon; Part III: The Televised Debates. U.S.G.P.O., 1961–1962.

This is the most complete record of the Kennedy-Nixon campaign speeches and debates. Though much too long for the general reader, this work will prove useful to the student of political debate, communication analysis, campaigning, and Americana. Questions of the alarmist nature of Kennedy's campaign or of the overly folksy nature of Nixon's political approach, as well as the degree to which regionalism has declined as a factor in American politics, can all be researched here.

Nixon, Richard M., *Six Crises*. New York: Doubleday, 1962, 460 pp. See entry annotated under section entitled "Critics: Gentle and Severe."

Kraus, Sidney, ed. *The Great Debates: Background, Perspective, Effects*. Bloomington, Indiana: Indiana University Press, 1962. 439 pp.

Here are the texts of the four famous TV debates between Kennedy and Nixon. Included is a discussion of the difficulty of textual accuracy (which was not found to be a crucial issue), and of the debates' impact on public opinion. Kraus quotes a Kennedy statement which reveals the successful candidate's zest for the TV medium (Kennedy eagerly anticipated televised debates with Goldwater), together with some of his suggestions for modification. Nixon, in a letter to Kraus, expressed a more reserved view: "What we need now is a close and careful estimate of their precise effect on the election returns and, on this basis, a sober judgment of their worth and future status." Comments by authorities on communications and public opinion are also included.

Since Kraus' work, two Ph.D. theses have appeared on this subject, one concluding that Kennedy gained ground because of the debates, the other holding that the debates made little difference.

Adlai Stevenson was probably correct when he suggested, after discussing possible Vice Presidential running mates with Sargent Shriver in 1956, that Kennedy's clean-cut "All-American Boy" appearance and sincerity would contrast favorably with the heavier-featured Nixon.

Smith, David S. *Alfred E. Smith and John Kennedy: The Religious Issue During the Presidential Campaigns of 1928 and 1960.* Unpublished Ph.D. Dissertation, Southern Illinois University, 1964. Available from University Microfilms, Inc., Ann Arbor, Michigan.

Many writers indicate that the election of a Catholic President shows how much the country has changed since 1928. This careful, scholarly examination of both Catholic Presidential candidates disputes this point, and concludes that how the issue was handled by Smith and Kennedy was a more crucial factor than the disappearance of bigotry. Kennedy's approach, the author maintains, was far superior and less personal than Smith's. Smith "frequently withdrew in silence, while Kennedy chose to confront the issue head on. . . . Smith resorted to bitterness while Kennedy was able to maintain his composure and retort with skill," often turning the controversy to his advantage. It is of course possible to answer the author's argument by speculating that if the country had changed more by 1928 Smith might have been psychologically more able and politically more successful in dealing with the issue. But this comparison was worthwhile making.

Wicker, Tom, "Kennedy as a Public Speakah," *New York Times Magazine,* February 28, 1962, p. 14.

This reporter, who captures political color and personal foibles with unmatched accuracy, analyzes Kennedy's speaking style, and finds it to be quite formidable. "The President," writes Wicker,

> probably has no peer in the simple art of political exhortation. Whether he is talking about the economy, the space program, the minimum wage, Arizona's water problem or the Democratic party deficit, he can impart a messianic ring to his voice, a missionary zeal to his words, and a ringmaster's authority to his stabbing forefinger.

Powell, James Grant. *An Analytical and Comparative Study of the Persuasion of Kennedy and Nixon in the 1960 Campaign.*

Unpublished Ph.D. Dissertation, University of Wisconsin, 1963. 934 pp. Available from University Microfilms, Inc., Ann Arbor, Michigan.

For those who wish a more detailed study than Theodore White's *The Making of the President, 1960,* this scholar analyzes the campaign speeches of both candidates (though not the television debates) and the audience's reaction to them. The audience appeal of Nixon's speaking technique is revealed here better than in most writing about the campaign. Nevertheless, he concludes, "Kennedy's speeches were characterized by an economy of style; Nixon's by a simplicity of style and a lack of conciseness."

Because most newspapers are owned by Republicans, Nixon's speeches won greater editorial support than Kennedy's. The columnist employed by the newspapers for the most part gave their support to Kennedy, the Democrat.

Gray, Charles H. "A Scale Analysis of the Voting Records of Senators Kennedy, Johnson and Goldwater, 1957–1960," *American Political Science Review,* September, 1965, pp. 615–21.

Complete with charts, this is a complicated way of stating there was a difference between Kennedy, Johnson, and Goldwater when they voted on issues.

CHAPTER V.

Presidency: Actions, Policies, Politics, Administration, Associated Personalities

Neustadt, Richard E. *Presidential Power.* New York: John Wiley and Sons, Inc. 1960, 1964. Paperback ed., New York: New American Library, 1964. 221 pp.

    Written in 1959 by an academic political scientist with first-hand experience in the Truman and Kennedy Administrations, *Presidential Power* is a study of the implications of decision-making in the three Administrations prior to Kennedy's. Neustadt seems to conclude that a President cannot, after all, do very much, and furthermore, shouldn't feel sorry about it. It is very strange that critics consider Neustadt's book to be in the Machiavellian tradition of advising a ruler how to rule cunningly. Also, Kennedy's affinity for Neustadt's ideas might have caused enthusiastic supporters of Kennedy to scale down their expectations when he assumed the Presidency.

    Chapter 8 instructs a future President like Kennedy what the problems and potentials of the Presidency would be like in the 1960's. With no foreseeable possibility of institutional reform, the power of the President would continue to rest on his ability to persuade officials and politicians of whatever political persuasion that it was to their advantage to follow the President and also his policies. Once personally acquainted with Kennedy, Neustadt advised him to read particularly

102 THE KENNEDY LITERATURE

Chapter 3, "The Power to Persuade," and Chapter 7, "Men in Office." Neustadt prepared for Kennedy a paper on "Organizing the Transition" and also later memoranda on staffing the priority decisions to be made by the President-elect and future President. These papers will presumably be available in the Kennedy Library in Cambridge, Massachusetts, at which institution Neustadt is now director of the John F. Kennedy Institute of Politics.

The 1964 edition of *Presidential Power* contains a brief, brilliantly written analysis (in *"Afterword: 1964"*) of unique aspects of the Presidency at the end of the Kennedy Administration and the beginning of the Johnson era. Some of these aspects are also highly disturbing: "What a President now lives with," says Neustadt, "is the consequence of a substantial nuclear delivery capability acquired by the Soviet Union as well as the United States. It is the mutual capability which pushes our choice-making—and theirs, too, of course—into a new dimension of risk. In previous writings I have termed this the risk of 'irreversibility,' the risk that either bureaucratic momentum in a large-scale undertaking or mutual miscalculation by atomic adversaries, or both combined, may make it infeasible to call back, or play over, or revise an action taken in our foreign relations, at least within the range of the Cold War. But the term 'irreversibility,' standing alone, does not really suffice to convey what is new in this dimension. . . . Therefore, to amend the term: what is new since the Soviets acquired their missiles is the risk of *irreversibility become irreparable.*"

There is no question but that Neustadt's and Kennedy's administrative ideas were strikingly parallel, but Kennedy naturally wished to avoid any appearance of a Machiavellian adviser whispering suggestions in the prince's ear for the purposes of accumulating and manipulating power. According to Schlesinger, Kennedy was "a little annoyed by the notion that he was modelling his Presidency on the doctrines of *Presidential Power*. He once remarked that Neustadt 'makes everything a President does seem too premeditated.' "

Ross, Irwin, "The Men Around Kennedy," *New York Post,* October 3–7, 1960.

A reporter's portrait of the major aides in Kennedy's campaign of 1960 who continued with him in the White House. Ross highlights aspects of their political personalities not always touched upon by others. A Ross characteristic is to give *Post* readers a picture of just how "liberal" each aide is through quotes and just how (and this is very interestingly done in the case of Sorensen) the aid reconciles his liberal commitment, if any, with Kennedy's politics.

Henry, Laurin L., "The Transition: The New Administration," *The Presidential Election, and Transition, 1960–61.* **Edited by Paul T. David. Washington, D.C.: The Brookings Institution, 1961.**
Most writers on the Bay of Pigs disaster indulged in a remarkable degree of emotional sympathy for Kennedy; they attempted to hold on to their image of Kennedy as a strong person who made the big decisions himself, and at the same time to indicate that in the case of the Cuban invasion, the juggernaut was already rolling and that no one could be expected to stop it. In this article a political scientist sees more serious implications in the fiasco:

> Kennedy had surrounded himself, as he preferred, with more than one set of advisers, in a very fluid staff system, but apparently in the pinch, he had not asked the probing question himself or put together all of the pieces essential to a judgment and no one else had taken it on himself to do so.

Crown, James Tracy and George P. Penty, *Kennedy in Power.* **New York: Ballantine, 1961. 192 pp.**
This book begins with an analysis of the political implications of the first year of the Kennedy Administration in the areas of legislative-leadership, economic program and civil liberties. Then special attention is given to the Kennedy Administration's hopes for improved relations with developing lands and the overwhelming obstacles to these aspirations. Later, fundamental questions are raised concerning either the desirability or feasibility of Kennedy's call for a race to the moon, his civil defense program, and his emphasis on "green beret" counterguerrilla forces. The book specifically assesses responsibility for the Bay of Pigs fiasco.

Also in the area of foreign policy, the work examines the tension between two basic convictions of Kennedy, that "only when our arms are sufficient beyond doubt can we be certain beyond doubt that they will never be employed"; that because of the nature of the arms race itself conflicting groups of nations are "racing to alter that uncertain balance of terror that stays the hand of mankind's final war."

A final section takes the long view of Kennedy as a skillful leader trapped in working the machinery of national sovereignty in an age when national sovereignty had become increasingly obsolete. Here Kennedy is regarded as the child of an age, in the words of Matthew Arnold, "between two worlds—one dead, the other powerless to be born."

A biographical note on Professor Crown is presented on p. 175 of this bibliography. George Penty is an editor and writer in New York City.

For reasons which will be obvious, the author of this critical biography has chosen to cite the reviews by others of his own work:

> One of the first books to attempt an assessment of John F. Kennedy's Administration and to raise the question of whether there had been a change in the concept of the Presidential office since his inauguration. . . . While generally approving of the President, the authors concluded that machinery is not so important as personality and 'style' and that during the first year of the new Administration it had become clear that Senator Kennedy would have been the first to criticize President Kennedy because 'practical' considerations had sometimes led to major contradictions and serious errors. This differed from the view of a number of other writers, who were more inclined to attribute errors to faulty machinery rather than to mistakes in judgment or lapses in consistency. Marshall E. Dimock, *Encyclopedia Britannica Book of the Year, 1962,* p. 555.

> The book is in fact a shrewd, thoughtful, informed essay on the achievements and failings of the first year. 'Critical and skeptical analysis' is accurate enough, but 'frightening contradictions' turn out to be a number of dualisms the authors find in the President (much like those found in most activist Presidents). . . . In between these findings are a host of penetrating judgments on specific policies and episodes. . . . Both Kennedy and Khrushchev, they conclude in a typically shrewd observation, 'by the requirements of their recruitment to high office have a high degree of emotional commitment to the slogans of their power systems.' Kennedy, they imply, must break out of his dualism and ambivalence if he is to master the forces confronting him. Such responsible criticism is badly needed, yet there is a curiously two-

dimensional quality about *Kennedy in Power*. Missing are the sweat and shoving, the babble and confusion and lunging ambitions in the midst of which the business of politics is actually conducted.

Still, this book, like the others, was written in the middle of the journey. It is the best analysis we shall have for some time of the anatomy of Kennedy policies. It also provides a fascinating balance sheet of the intellectuals' hopes and misgivings as President Kennedy ends his first year. James MacGregor Burns, "Kennedy's First Year," *Nation,* January 6, 1963, pp. 14–15.

Phillips, Cabell, "Kennedy's Vast Patronage Major Lever on Congress," *The New York Times,* February 19, 1961, pp. 1 f.

One of the few specific discussions of the approximately 100 major policy-making appointments, and other appointments—totalling about 4,000—which the President uses in an attempt to build up his own political organization (since his control over the sprawling, 50-state Democratic parties comprising the national Democratic Party is most uncertain) and to strengthen his shaky influence on Congress. Author Phillips is a first-rate *Times* political reporter and interpreter. Using hindsight, a reader can see that the article exaggerates the effectiveness of Presidential patronage in getting things done. To an impressive extent Kennedy made key appointments on a basis of estimated competence rather than as a political reward.

Schnapper, B. N., ed. *New Frontiers of the Kennedy Administration: Texts of the Task Force Reports prepared for the President.* Washington: Public Affairs Press, 1961. 170 pp.

Were distinguished authorities and public figures enticed by Kennedy to submit reports to him suggesting specific policies and organization for the purpose of publicity alone—being a kind of honorific patronage—or did he seriously intend to use them? His major biographers indicate he took them seriously, but no one has yet matched the suggestions with subsequent actions with sufficient care to be able to give a convincing estimate of the usefulness of such reports for future "transitions" of administrations. These reports, some of them presenting a high level of judgment and insight provide a good beginning for such an evaluation.

Sanghvi, Ramesh. *John F. Kennedy: A Political Biography.* Bombay: Perennial Press, 1961. 200 pp. Foreword by V. K. Krishna Menon.

An example of the widespread interest in Kennedy abroad, this favorable general account of Kennedy's political history and policies was written by an intelligent leftwing Indian lawyer-journalist. Krishna Menon's lengthy foreword is of interest not because he says much about Kennedy, whom he little admired, but because of his comments on American political institutions. This title is available in the Library of Congress.

"Role of Robert Kennedy; No. 2 Man in Washington," *U.S. News and World Report,* July 19, 1961, pp. 42–45.

Just as *Look* became a magazine which was usually most helpful to President Kennedy's career, so *U.S. News and World Report* became identified as a publication which most consistently needled and questioned him and his policies. In the area of factual reporting it carried an interesting series of articles treating the relationship of John and Robert Kennedy, the tasks undertaken by Robert, the power he accumulated, and views Washington figures expressed about Robert and his relationship with his brother. The piece cited deals with Robert's tasks and growing influence. A much earlier piece in this magazine on the John and Robert team was "The Kennedy Brothers Off to a Fast Start," April 12, 1957, pp. 77–79. Later stories in the magazine sequence were "Bobby Kennedy: Is He 'Assistant President'?" pp. 48–52, and "Power of the Kennedy Brothers: A Comparison with other First Families," July 16, 1962, pp. 56–59. The same magazine gave Robert a chance to explain at length his role and his brother's policies in "Robert Kennedy Speaks His Mind: Interview," January 28, 1963, pp. 54–65.

Blum, J. M., "Kennedy's Ten Foot Shelf," *New York Times Magazine,* March 12, 1961, p. 264.

. . . One of the best brief expositions of Kennedy's search for "actionable ideas," what he read at the beginning of his Administration, and how he related his reading to the formation of programs. Many of the authors whom he read served as advisers, both in and out of government.

Alsop, Stewart, "White House Insiders," *Saturday Evening Post,* June 10, 1961, pp. 19 f.

A writer and editor for the *Saturday Evening Post,* the abler Alsop in Washington presents a penetrating and concise sketch of the major Kennedy White House aides, a few of the President's advisers and friends, and some of their inter-relationships. In retrospect, Alsop's analysis held up very well during the Kennedy tenure, although some of the clashes which Alsop reasoned were certain to erupt either did not become public or were diffused by Kennedy's own skillful management. Alsop, incidentally, credits gadfly and idea man W. W. Rostow of M.I.T. with giving Kennedy the phrase "this country is ready to get moving again."

Carleton, William Graves, "The Cult of Personality Comes to the White House," *Harper's* Magazine, December, 1961, pp. 63–68.

Carleton is one of the few highly skilled political scientist-historians who asks and answers the hard questions about his subject. The article is not a personal attack upon Kennedy or his motives, but an examination of the reasons for and consequences of a President's attempt to gain nomination, win the election, and then to govern through the elaborate projection of personal magnetism rather than through guiding a coalition of powerful political leaders in Congress, the Administration, and the Democratic Party. The institutional consequences of appointing a Cabinet largely of competent technicians who have little political standing is also touched upon. These important ideas are not fully worked out, although they are again touched upon in a later *Antioch Review* article by the same author cited elsewhere in the bibliography. Such an important study deserves further development either by Carleton or other political analysts.

One paragraph throws a particularly revealing light upon the entire Kennedy performance:

> Much of his astonishing activity—official and personal—has grown out of a conscious effort to overcome the handicaps of his youthfulness, his close election, and his lack of conspicuous political achievement or the kind of prestige which brings general and automatic acceptance of his leadership.

Hoopes, Roy. *What the President Does All Day.* New York: John Day, 1962. 64 pp.

On a particularly dull day for newsmen covering the White House, several of them pumped Caroline Kennedy about her father's activities in his office and received this scoop: "Oh, he's just sitting in there with his shoes off doing nothing." It was a busier day that Hoopes illustrates, with interesting photographs and brief text. The book is especially evocative of the White House command post when read with Jim Bishop's chronicle, *A Day in the Life of President Kennedy.*

Neustadt, Richard E., "Approaches to Staffing the Presidency: Notes on FDR and JFK," *American Political Science Review,* December, 1963, pp. 855–62.

When Professor Neustadt submitted to candidate Kennedy in the closing days of the 1960 Presidential campaign a report on the staffing problems facing a new President, Kennedy was particularly fascinated with the way Franklin Roosevelt solved *his* staffing problems. In this work, which was written before Kennedy's death (though published afterwards), Neustadt authoritatively shows how although Kennedy inherited much of the staff apparatus created by Roosevelt, Kennedy's Presidency lacked the political background of urgency which facilitated Roosevelt's ability to get results from this system. In addition to indicating similarities with Roosevelt, Neustadt carefully delineates the administrative techniques which were peculiar to Kennedy. He fails to make clear, however, why Kennedy's cabinet and staff seemed so drab and colorless in comparison with Roosevelt's, although Neustadt's own advice for a President to keep tight control of his staff would tend to make such an event likely.

Sorensen, Theodore. *Decision-Making in the White House.* Introduction by John F. Kennedy. New York: Columbia University Press, 1963. 94 pp.

From a series of very restrained and very academic lectures given at Columbia University, the President's top administrative aide elaborates on the theme Kennedy sets out in the introduction: the problem of the gap between a President's aspirations and what he can actually do.

Graff, Henry F. "Preserving the Secrets of the White House," *New York Times Magazine,* December 29, 1963, pp. 9 f.

Historian Henry Graff of Columbia University provides an authoritative and readable general view of the disposition of the President's papers during his tenure and after he leaves the White House and the reasoning behind these practices. The President's public papers are published in annual volumes throughout his tenure and include Presidential Proclamations, Messages and Reports to Congress and, sometimes, Executive Orders. However, a considerable number of interesting items are his personal papers and belong solely "to him or his survivors to be disposed of or even destroyed" as he or they see fit. This tradition, which does not apply equally to cabinet officers, is well established and goes unchallenged in the case of the President. Included as private papers (most of Kennedy's will be available in the Kennedy Library) are diaries (if any) and personal notes, drafts of policy proposals, interoffice memoranda, position papers and staff reports. Kennedy kept no diary and aide memoirs and, "despite the urging of his friends and associates he never systematically committed his private observations to paper." This article should be read before a visit to the National Archives in Washington, D.C., or to the Kennedy Library in Cambridge, Massachusetts.

Cater, Douglass. *Power in Washington.* New York: Random House, Inc., 1964. 275 pp.

Perhaps the very best readable and sound book about the network of power in Washington with which Kennedy had to struggle. From the viewpoint of Washington as a whole, the power of the Presidency, and particularly the Kennedy Presidency, shrinks amazingly as compared with White House-oriented studies. Cater's *forte* is that he can cut through the artificial and institutional categories which often prevent academic studies from picturing Washington as it really operates. The author's insight benefits from years of experience as political writer, Washington editor of the *Reporter,* and high level government adviser—the latter role unfortunately and occasionally restricting him to unnecessary caution in expression. This report helps the reader understand what happened to Kennedy's legislative program; like most such books, however, it is overly generous in attributing Kennedy's legislative weakness to forces entirely beyond human control.

The author's openminded awareness of this problem is cogently discussed in Chapter 4, which provides a useful analysis of the problems involved in making a judgment about the Kennedy Administration.

Koenig, Louis. *The Chief Executive.* New York: Harcourt, Brace and World, 1964. 435 pp.

A good starting point for research on the Kennedy Administration, and written mainly during the Kennedy years, this work contains many examples of Kennedy's views and actions in the office of President. Written by a New York University political scientist who is an established authority on the Presidency, the book covers the major constitutional, political, and personal aspects of the office. A careful reading of this work, which stresses the continuity of the office, will save the student of any one Administration from a parochial exaggeration of the effect that any one President (even a two-term one) can have on the Presidency of the country, much less on the world as a whole. The book is objectively written. Although its author is an admitted advocate of a strong Chief Executive, he understands the Eisenhower Administration, and, in this work the change from the Eisenhower Administration to the Kennedy Administration does not seem as abrupt as in most of the Kennedy literature.

Schreiber, G. R. *The Bobby Baker Affair.* Chicago: Henry Regnery Company, 1964. 190 pp.

Most of the accounts of the Kennedy period tend to ignore the surrounding politics of Washington and the country to such an extent that it is almost possible to believe Kennedy's politics began and ended within the circle of top advisers in the Executive branch. It is important to recognize that, like Truman and Eisenhower, Kennedy hoped to improve the seamier side of American political life. In this book the editor of *Vend,* the trade magazine of the vending machine industry, on basis of first-hand inquiry and extensive use of the records of the Senate Rules Committee, attempts to piece together the strands of the career of Bobby Baker, Secretary of the Senate majority, protégé of Lyndon Johnson (Baker won the name of "Little Lyndon" on Capitol Hill) and operator extraordinary. The unusual work in Washington performed by Grant Stockdale (a suicide), Al Novak (a suicide), and Carol Tyler, victim of a small plane crash, are either touched upon or examined at some length. Likewise, the work of Fred B. Black, Jr. and Thomas Webb as well as the interests of the Texan multi-millionaire Murchison brothers in Washington are explored. These characters are all worth knowing about in terms of the politics of the time.

Schreiber's book is expose writing but it is not wild or vitriolic, and stays so close to public evidence that it is sometimes dull. Sometimes, too, the connections between persons and events are insufficiently clarified. The book is not well organized and its style is quite dry, for example, the following paragraph:

> The fact that Reynolds [a witness against Baker] brought Johnson's name squarely into the Baker affair may have contributed to reports that there was a "dump Lyndon" movement afoot. When Reynolds first told the press about his insurance on the life of Johnson, LBJ was Vice-President. By the time Reynolds was called before the Senate Rules Committee, which heard his testimony behind closed doors for two days, a great and terrible change had taken place. President Kennedy had been assassinated and Lyndon B. Johnson had moved into the White House.

At his last press conference, November 14, 1963, President Kennedy remarked:

> Mr. Baker is now being investigated, and I think we will know a good deal more about Mr. Baker before we are through. Other people may be investigated as time goes on. . . .

All in all, governmental standards in Washington under the Kennedy Administration compared quite favorably with state and municipal governments in other parts of America. For the attempts of President Johnson's White House aides to discredit Reynolds' testimony, see *The New York Times,* February 8, 1964, pp. 1 ff.

Harris, Seymour F. *The Economics of the Kennedy Years and a Look Ahead.* New York: Harper & Row, 1964. 273 pp.

This Harvard economist, who was a particularly helpful adviser to Senator Kennedy's campaign for reviving the New England economy, was very familiar with theories, forces, and personalities which figured in Kennedy's surprisingly bitter economic struggles as President.

Harris writes perceptively and objectively about how economic policy was formulated under Kennedy. He is a liberal economist, but not a polemicist.

Congress and Nation 1945-1965: A Review of Government and Politics in the Post War Years. Washington, D. C.: Congressional Quarterly, 1964. 1,784 pp.

For the researchers who use its table of contents and index carefully, this is by far the most useful compendium and analysis of Kennedy's relations with Congress and the general politics of the Kennedy years. A student using this work can also trace the fate of Kennedy's legislation during his Presidency.

Crown, James Tracy, "President Kennedy—As the World Knew Him," *Coronet* Magazine, January, 1964, pp. 18–25.

Written before Kennedy's assassination, although published just afterward, this falls into the category of "Kennedy Without Tears" pieces which confirms the remarkable esteem in which Kennedy was held abroad. The article explains how Kennedy moved, in a short time, from a virtual unknown to become for foreigners one of the most popular Americans in history. Some mention is made of the dangers of the contemporary trend to have the entire United States symbolized to the world in terms of the personality of its President, with an extra reminder that a John Kennedy would not always turn up as President. This is a popular article based largely on the author's first-hand observations in Europe, Africa, and Asia. However, the extraordinary appeal of Kennedy across national boundaries (it penetrated especially strongly into Communist countries) is a phenomenon meriting more searching study.

Subsequent to this article, the author, traveling in late 1967 in villages of Nepal, saw pictures of John F. Kennedy on walls of homes and small bookstores. In Moscow in early 1968 he found public expression of admiration for Kennedy to be greater even than it had been before.

Bundy, McGeorge, "The President and the Peace," *Foreign Affairs,* April, 1964, pp. 354–65.

Any Bundy article is a helpful clue to this extremely important Kennedy adviser whose role in the Administration seldom comes through clearly in the Kennedy literature. He long shared Kennedy's near obsession with military diplomacy. He calls the American Presidency the world's best hope for preventing nuclear war. He praises the skill, responsibility, and restraint of President Kennedy during the Cuban missile crisis and his astuteness in achieving the nuclear test ban treaty. Bundy's formula for peace is for the United States to maintain strategic superiority over the Soviet Union. Joseph Kraft has a useful profile of Bundy in his *Profiles in Power.*

Falk, S. L., "The National Security Council under Truman, Eisenhower and Kennedy," *Political Science Quarterly*, September 1964, pp. 403–34.

A careful student of the National Security Council gives a careful comparison of the different uses various Presidents have made of a single institution. He shows how Kennedy kept some of Truman's informality and used some of Eisenhower's institutionalization of procedures but established much more flexibility in procedures than did Eisenhower. Falk's estimate of the usefulness of the National Security Council, whose need he states is "self evident," is not fully borne out in the case of the Kennedy Administration, according to evidence by Kennedy partisans Sorensen and Schlesinger.

Cornwell, Elmer E., Jr. *Presidential Leadership of Public Opinion.* Bloomington, Indiana: Indiana University Press, 1965. 369 pp.

A latter section of this survey of various Presidents draws conclusions from some of the pertinent writing about Kennedy's speaking techniques, press relations, and, especially, the use of television. The book is generally descriptive rather than analytical. It is obvious that further and deeper research in this area should be attempted by students of communications and journalism.

Neustadt, Richard E. "Statement of Richard E. Neustadt, Professor of Government, Columbia University, March 25, 1963," pp. 74–103. *Administration of National Security: Staff Reports and Hearings.* U.S. Senate, Subcommittee on National Security Staffing and Operations of the Committee on Government

114 THE KENNEDY LITERATURE

Operations. Eighty-Eighth Congress. Washington: U.S. Government Printing Office, 1965.

Richard Neustadt, political scientist and Presidential adviser, here gives one of the most authoritative analytical surveys of the problems President Kennedy faced in attempting to administer foreign affairs and international security affairs. Some of his section titles are revealing: "The President as Risktaker," "The President Versus Officialdom," "Officialdom Versus the President," "Help from the Secretary of State?" and "The Secretary Versus the Others." There follows a period of questioning of Neustadt by Senators and Staff members in which the tendency of the Secretary of Defense, Treasury, and others to run their own independent foreign policy is touched upon interestingly, but too briefly. Neustadt believes, as did President Kennedy whom he advised, "the most effective kind of staff organization is an organization built around what I would call an action forcing process, by which I mean a steady stream of actionable issues, concrete issues, that have to be attended to, issues where something has to be done, a decision has to be reached." Policy was defined by Neustadt as a "crystalization of a series of concrete decisions. Everything else I would call 'aspiration.' " In reading the Kennedy literature one concludes that the key to the great weaknesses as well as the technical strength of the Kennedy administration is found in the President's sharing of Neustadt's administrative concepts.

Neustadt has adapted this testimony into an intellectually sparkling "Afterword" for the 1964 edition of his excellent book, *Presidential Power;* this latter volume is more easily attainable, but the reader desiring a sophisticated, high-level understanding of Kennedy's problems in administering national security affairs, the area of his greatest fiascos and triumphs, will have to turn to this important Senate document.

Kennedy, John F. *Kennedy and the Press: The News Conferences.* Edited and Annotated by Harold W. Chase and Allen H. Lerman. Introduction by Pierre Salinger. New York: Thomas Y. Crowell Company, 1965. 555 pp.

In a very informative introduction about Kennedy and the press, former presidential press secretary Salinger makes a persuasive case for his view that lacking the memoirs the President would surely have written had he lived, and in view of what we know of the number of minds that participated in Presidential speech writing and the drafting of official papers, the texts of the press conferences are undoubtedly the most revelatory of his legacies.

Of course Kennedy had a morning of briefing for these conferences which included practice questions and answers, and no one has ever denied an occasional planted question crept into the actual conference. Nevertheless, the cogency, relevance, style, and charm are clearly Kennedy's own.

The press conference was undoubtedly Kennedy's greatest medium for reaching the public. His first performance had sixty-five million listeners, and he thereafter averaged eighteen million. Besides the Kennedy wit, the reader will find the frustrating mixture of candor and evasiveness which accompanies public life.

On rare occasions a memorable unguarded phrase would pop out, as in his response to a question regarding racial division in the country. "Over the long run we are going to have a mix. This will be true racially, socially, ethnically, geographically, and that is really, finally, the best way," Kennedy replied.

In print the substance of the performances is much less winning than one recalled it as being, but there is enough here to show how the young President with the remarkable memory and "apparent frankness" captured the public's imagination.

Before the listing, in chronological order, of the press conferences, the editors give a brief summary of relevant events which provoked certain questions. They also add an occasional footnote, but give little critical evaluation of the accuracy or completeness of the various Kennedy responses. The scholars' task is made easier by the inclusion of a very helpful index. Most of the televised press conferences, incidentally, will be available for the researcher at the Kennedy Library in Cambridge, Massachusetts.

Mahajani, Usha. "Kennedy and the Strategy of Aid: The Clay Report and After." *Western Political Quarterly,* September, 1965.

This is a political scientist's analysis of an "Establishment" type committee, appointed by Kennedy, whose report was in many ways hostile toward aspects of Kennedy's foreign aid concepts, and caused difficulty for his foreign aid program. Kennedy's reliance upon the type of political leader like General Lucius Clay is brought into question by the evidence. The analysis is generally objective.

Abel, Elie. *The Missile Crisis.* Philadelphia: Lippincott, 1966. 220 pp. Paperback ed., New York: Bantam Books, 1966. 208 pp.

Abel, for 10 years a correspondent for *The New York Times* and now an NBC correspondent with good contacts at Defense and State Departments presents a carefully worded but interesting day-by-day account of the developments in the Cuban missile crisis. A reader cannot be certain whether Abel has the final word regarding episodes about which there are various versions, but the author's general outline of the decision-making process involved checks out with the best scholarly research on the subject. On the other hand, the scholarly researchers often did not have access to the interviews Abel achieved. The President's creation and use of ExCom is interestingly told, although its long-run implications are not explored.

What the Cuban missile crisis reveals for those who did not already know it is that international politics is often conducted in an irresponsible and irrational way. Neither Kennedy nor Khrushchev created this gambling table situation, but faced with it, Kennedy behaved in a careful and rather sophisticated manner. Abel's account shows there was much more traditional diplomacy going on than some of the more sensational and hair-raising versions of the encounter indicate.

Baker, Leonard. *The Johnson Eclipse: A President's Vice-Presidency.* New York: MacMillan, 1966. 282 pp.

A rather general reporter's review of the activities of a Vice President whose chief wanted him to be informed about what was going on, but who relied on him more for support than advice. Johnson's exhilarating trips abroad, when the Vice President shook hands, gave away ball point pens, and talked quite seriously with foreign leaders, is described. Throughout John Kennedy seemed to have had more respect both for the person and for the political astuteness of the Vice President than did his brother Robert. Evelyn Lincoln's *Kennedy and*

Johnson indicates there was more to the dump Johnson movement Leonard Baker discusses than this newsman was able to dig out.

Jacobson, Harold K. and Stein, Eric. *Diplomats, Scientists and Politicians: The U.S. and the Nuclear Test Ban Negotiations.* Ann Arbor, Michigan: University of Michigan Press, 1966. 538 pp.

A complex unraveling of the factors which were ultimately responsible for Kennedy's nuclear test ban treaty. The President's relations with his scientific adviser Jerome Weisner are particularly important. A careful reading of such books as this one is essential before generalizations can validly be made about the achievements of the Kennedy Administration and the efforts that were required to achieve them. The authors make it quite clear that it was the advent of the Kennedy Administration which gave the great impetus to the push for a test ban. The latter section of the book and the index will direct the reader to Kennedy's contribution.

Evans, Rowland and Novak, Robert, *Lyndon B. Johnson: The Exercise of Power.* New York: New American Library, 1966. 574 pp.

These two journalists are outstanding for digging out facts overlooked by others. They are not particularly outstanding in terms of insight or judgment. The wealth of pertinent factual material they weave together here, however, make this a very important book for those concerned with the relations of John Kennedy and Lyndon Johnson in the Senate, during their competition for the nomination, and Johnson's troubled vice-presidency. The authors are first rate in coverage of legislative maneuvering, a vital arena of policy making which too many reporters ignore in favor of the more glamorous office of President. They develop one of the best available portraits of Johnson's political shrewdness, at the same time objectively exposing startling areas of political weakness certain to cause him future peril.

Kraft, Joseph. *Profiles in Power: A Washington Insight.* New York: New American Library, 1966. 192 pp.

Kraft was a confidant of Kennedy and one of the most perceptive of the few Washington writers who forthrightly attempt to measure men against the institutions and offices they inhabit. Most of the eighteen serious magazine pieces in this collection deal directly with, or have direct bearing upon, the Kennedy Administration. Kraft gives a good picture of the radical changes McNamara introduced, although he fails to explore deeply enough the later implications of McNamara's moving into foreign policy.

The author's portrait is one of the few which made McGeorge Bundy an understandable human being—not a likeable one, but to Kraft, admirable. The analysis of Dean Rusk and the State Department's slowness seems harsh but there is little question but that this disappointment with Rusk was shared in the highest White House quarters. There is enough material here to start some serious rethinking about Kennedy's supposed reputation for always finding the right man for the right spot.

Fritchey, Clayton, "A Tale of One City and Two Men," *Harper's Magazine,* December, 1966, pp. 108–13.

This thoughtful and erudite columnist, a former aide to Adlai Stevenson, here contrasts what he contends were the halcyon days of forward looking policy in the Washington of Kennedy with the allegedly reckless and self-righteous policies of Johnson's Capitol. He specifically challenges President Johnson's claim to be carrying on Kennedy's policies in foreign affairs. "Never during his entire career," Kennedy partisan Fritchey writes, "Did President Kennedy put any region of the world ahead of Europe." Both Kennedy's brothers continue to advocate this policy, Fritchey maintains, while Johnson has succeeded in placing one million men under Pacific Headquarters. In this article and in his newspaper columns he is severely critical of Secretary of State Dean Rusk and maintains that he would have had to follow a different policy under the Kennedy Administration. Numerous other writers on the Johnson Administration, including his more admiring biographers, stress the continuity of Eisenhower-Kennedy-Johnson foreign policy.

Hilsman, Roger. *To Move a Nation: The Politics of Foreign Policy in the Administration of John F. Kennedy.* New York: Doubleday, 1967. 602 pp.

This work by a professor who was an official in the State Department during the Kennedy Administration has the solid quality of being about the subject matter of its title. Certain of the institutions—particularly in State, Defense, intelligence and the White House—personalities and forces at home and abroad which shaped policies, are perceptively and interestingly depicted. Asian policy questions, Hilsman's specialty, are particularly well developed. There is genuinely new information and interpretation here.

Being in the bureaucracy beyond the White House, the author is less swayed by personal enthusiasm for Kennedy than was Sorensen or Schlesinger, and, therefore, the even handed credit he gives Kennedy for many coherent and perceptive decisions in the area of foreign policy are all the more interesting. The book is also very well written, the soundness of many of its judgments will be of lasting value, and it deserves wider and more serious study than has been given it in comparison to less analytical works of similar subject matter.

Lincoln, Evelyn. *Kennedy and Johnson.* New York: Holt, Rhinehart and Winston, 1968. 207 pp.

In a much more political book than her *My Twelve Years with John F. Kennedy,* President Kennedy's personal secretary draws on first hand observations, her diaries, and other records to suggest that there was not only a great difference in style between the two men, but that this difference was more basic and reveals an ultimate difference in substance between the two Presidencies. An undisguised partisan of her former boss, she nonetheless gives Vice President Johnson credit for working hard for Kennedy in the 1960 campaign in the South, in two administrative councils, and some missions abroad. But she challenges other versions of their bond at the Democratic Convention of 1960, Johnson's work for Kennedy's legislative program, his growth and his usefulness as a figure with top level national responsibilities. Sprinkled with a good deal of humor and some caustic "put downs" of Johnson, the book shows the early struggle between the two Democratic candidates, the scars left by it, the tasks the President assigned Vice President Johnson, gives an estimate of mediocre performance by Johnson and indicates that because of this lackluster performance, coupled with Johnson's failure to end Texas political quarreling, and the threatening "Bobby Baker" scandal, about which Kennedy knew more than the general public, Kennedy had decided to replace Johnson with North Carolina Governor Terry Sanford at the 1964 Democratic Convention. This decision, Evelyn Lincoln states, President Kennedy confided to her in her office a few days before leaving for his fatal trip to Johnson's home state. Here the book abruptly ends, leaving urgent questions dangling in the air.

Rumors of a "dump Johnson movement" in late 1963 had never been adequately researched at the time because the impact of the Baker scandal was not yet measured, because Kennedy at his press conferences had discouraged such speculation, and because the final decision would be his alone. The material in her book along with her established reputation for veracity led most reviewers to accept the author's report of President Kennedy's conversation. Some suggested Kennedy may have been merely exploding from a moment of pique —although the text clearly indicates otherwise—and many newsmen found it difficult to accept the possibility that they had missed the biggest story of Kennedy's last months in office. Senator Robert Kennedy in early 1968, while still supporting President Johnson's bid for reelection denied any knowledge of his brother's plan to drop Johnson in 1964, but in mid March, after his decision to challenge Johnson for the nomination, he invited Mrs. Lincoln to join his campaign.

Wicker, Tom. *JFK and LBJ: The Influence of Personality in Politics.* New York: William Morrow and Co., 1968. 297 pp.

A major political writer for *The New York Times* who observed and reported both Presidents with considerable insight shows how Kennedy, who believed in solid legislative achievement as a measure of success, got his program bogged down in Congress and how President Johnson, who swore by consensus, succeeded in dividing the country, at least temporarily, over the conduct of the Vietnam War. In both instances he demonstrates that the kind of men they were had an important bearing on their successes and failures. Other books which make some comparison of Kennedy and Johnson, although this is not their central concern, and whose titles reveal their slants, are Eric Goldman, *The Tragedy of Lyndon Johnson,* New York: Alfred A. Knopf, Inc., 1968; Hugh Sidey, *A Very Personal Presidency,* New York: Atheneum, 1968.

For a Johnson partisan who denounces Kennedy "cultists" who allegedly use the Kennedy legend to detract from President Johnson's accomplishments, see the columns of William White.

Kimball, Penn. *Bobby Kennedy and the New Politics.* Englewood Cliffs, New Jersey: Prentice-Hall, 1968. 301 pp.

A perceptive journalist makes a serious case for the view that John Kennedy ushered in a new kind of politics wherein a candidate speaks directly and frankly to youth encouraging hope but not propounding easy solutions or traditional cliches. The book deals centrally with Robert Kennedy, not John, but it states clearly and unsentimentally a case for major contribution by John Kennedy to American political campaigning and leadership and to reconciliation of age groups in politics. It is a thesis which is subject to proof, disproof, or modification during the present period of politics and thus, it is particularly fascinating for students of the present political flux.

Liang, Margaret. *The Next Kennedy.* New York: Coward McCann, 1968. 320 pp.

Part of this book summarizes the team work of John and Robert Kennedy and also gives some detailed attention to Robert's work as attorney general. Otherwise the work by a profilist for the *Times* of London sticks to its publisher's description as "a woman's view of Robert F. Kennedy as Prospective President." Also, see Timmisch's work on Robert Kennedy cited in a previous section.

CHAPTER VI.

Relations With Groups of Citizens

Knebel, Fletcher, "Democratic Forecast: A Catholic in 1960," *Look,* March 3, 1959, pp. 13–18 ff.

    This article contains Kennedy's most important statement on the necessity of separation of Church and State. Responding to Knebel's question, the then Senator Kennedy replied off the cuff:

> Whatever one's religion in his private life may be, for the officeholder nothing takes precedence over his oath to uphold the Constitution and all its parts—including the First Amendment and the strict separation of church and state. Without reference to the presidency, I believe as a senator that the separation of church and state is fundamental to our American concept and heritage and should remain so . . . There can be no question of Federal Funds being used for support of parochial or private schools. It's unconstitutional under the First Amendment as interpreted by the Supreme Court . . . As for such fringe matters as buses, lunches and other services, the issue is primarily social and economic and not religious. Each case must be judged on its merits within the law as interpreted by the courts.

Kennedy's numerous speeches to groups of ministers were simply a variation on this statement. The article is intended to disprove the contention, attributed to such influential Democrats as Speaker Sam Rayburn and former President Truman, that a Catholic on the ticket would arouse Protestant suspicion and lose the party votes. Mrs. Eleanor Roosevelt was also included among the doubters; in February, 1959, she stated elsewhere:

> I had hoped that the first President who was elected and was a Roman Catholic would be one who we felt certain had the character to separate church and state completely, and I have been simply worried because I had not been sure that Senator Kennedy could do that.

"Union Leaders Size up Kennedy and Johnson," *U.S. News and World Report,* July 11, 1960, pp. 96–99.

Most union leaders never forgot Senator Johnson's vote for the Taft-Hartley Act. But since he was majority leader of the party they generally supported, they soft pedaled their reservations, just as they did their reservations about Senator Kennedy's role in development of what turned out to be the Landrum Griffin Act placing restrictions on certain union practices. Most union leaders rejected Nixon as anti-labor and expressed enthusiasm for candidate Kennedy.

"Meany, Kennedy Discuss the 1960 Election Issues," *American Federationist,* November, 1960, pp. 12–20.

This extended expression of mutual admiration covers a number of areas of agreement between the AFL-CIO leadership and the Democratic candidate such as defense, welfare, unions, and other economic issues. An example of labor techniques of helping a Democratic candidate, among its members, without violating the Taft-Hartley Act provision against direct political expenditures.

McConnell, Grant. *Steel and the Presidency, 1962.* New York: W. W. Norton and Company, 1963. 115 pp.

Professor McConnell of the University of Chicago, author of a previous case study of the seizure of steel mills by the United States Government in 1951 under the direction of Truman, here examines, with somewhat surprising results, the politics and economics of Kennedy's efforts to roll back the steel price increase of 1962. Much of his work stems from interviews which, in order to protect sources, he unfortunately does not cite; nor does McConnell give any footnotes or bibliography. He seems inadequately to measure the cost to Kennedy of alienating the business community largely through abusive language. McConnell concludes that Kennedy gave "a virtuoso performance of simulating action and the situation was successfully disguised . . . Events rescued the President. Nevertheless, the administration's venture was perilously close to an exposure of impotence."

McConnell's case study tends to support Richard Neustadt's conclusion that the President's power, regardless of who holds that office, rests on much less solid ground and is much less powerful than generally realized.

For a factual resume of the Steel controversy see *New York Times,* April 23, 1962. For contrasting comments see "Kennedy—Business Feud Nears Peril Point," *Business Week,* July 7, 1962, pp. 92 f., and "Business Against Kennedy; A One Sided Hostility," *Round Table,* September, 1962, pp. 355 ff.

Blough, Roger Miles, "My Side of the Steel Price Story, As Told to Eleanor Harris," *Look,* January 29, 1963, pp. 19–23.

The article lives up to its self-explanatory title, with the head of the United States Steel Corporation's explanation of his surprise at Kennedy's hostile over-reaction to the steel industry's move for a reasonable profit. Blough points to dangers to economic freedom as well as individual liberty inherent in the retaliatory moves taken by President Kennedy and his aides.

Kempton, Murray, "Looking Back on the Anniversary," *Spectator,* December 1, 1963, p. 778.

A highly imaginative and interesting interpretation of Kennedy leaving Boston and then returning to unite in his person John Adams and the Boston Irish.

Golden, Harry. *Mr. Kennedy and the Negroes.* Cleveland: World Publishing Company, 1964. 319 pp.

A humane humorist and champion of both Kennedy and Negro rights in the South writes of the various phases and events marking Kennedy's relationship with Negroes. It also sheds light on the nature of Kennedy's political problems with Southern officials on integration.

Saunders, Doris, editor. *The Kennedy Years and the Negro: A Photographic Record.* Introduction by Andrew Hatcher. Chicago: Johnson Publishing Company, 1965. 143 pp.

The book includes photographs of Kennedy consulting with Negro leaders and campaigning among Negro citizens. A brief introduction by Kennedy's assistant press secretary discusses Kennedy's concern for Negroes and for civil rights. Unfortunately, there is nothing unexpected or revealing to be found in this work.

Kennedy, John F. *John F. Kennedy on Israel.* New York: Herzl Press, 1965. 62 pp.

This is a collection of the Kennedy statements as Senator and President regarding Israel and the United States' relations with that country.

Fuchs, Laurence. *John F. Kennedy and American Catholicism.* Meredith, 1967. 271 pp.

Kennedy's family, campaigns, and Presidency are placed against an historic background treatment of changing American attitudes toward Catholicism and Catholics, by a scholarly authority on religion in American politics. He presents a convincing argument that American attitudes have mellowed and that Kennedy helped bring this about, but he perhaps underestimates the significance that unlike 1928 the Democratic party nominated a Catholic whose image seemed very much like that of the contemporary "W.A.S.P." political leader.

CHAPTER VII.

Critics: Gentle and Severe

Roosevelt, Eleanor, "On My Own," *Saturday Evening Post,* March 8, 1958, pp. 32 ff.

The early reservations about Kennedy held by this powerful spokesman for liberal and idealistic Democrats are partially revealed in this article. Mrs. Roosevelt remained a thorn in Kennedy's side until she became an enthusiastic and genuine Kennedy supporter after his (and Nixon's) nomination. She reports her conclusion that even after talks with her friends and Kennedy himself, she remained convinced that Kennedy had not realized the importance of the McCarthy issue in the mid-1950's and that he had not taken the one conceivable stand on the issue which any man worthy of the Presidency must take. A headline on the piece, which was the concluding chapter of a serialization of Mrs. Roosevelt's book bearing the same title, read, "as for the current front-runner young Senator Kennedy, she takes a dim view of him." She took a much dimmer view of Nixon, whom she rated "a very able and very dangerous opportunist." Actually, the only reservation about Kennedy she expresses refers to the McCarthy question —which the Kennedy supporters thought was just so much water over the dam, but, which cast in the form of this article, was still able to make Stevensonians and a good many other liberals grit their teeth.

They could not find evidence to exclude Kennedy from Richard Rovere's sweeping conclusion about Senators and McCarthy: "The truth is," wrote political analyst Rovere, "that everyone in the Senate, or just about everyone, was scared stiff of him." Kennedy, incidentally, wrote an innocuous review of Rovere's book, *Senator Joe McCarthy*, for the *Washington Post*, June 28, 1959, p. E4.

Rayburn, Sam. "The Speaker Speaks of Presidents," *New York Times Magazine*, June 4, 1961, pp. 32 ff.

In this somewhat rambling but interesting reminiscence of eight Presidents with whom Rayburn had served (he did not serve "under" Presidents, he insists) Rayburn has something good to say about everyone including Warren Harding (Eisenhower was "a delightful personality, never offended many people"), but it is clear who he thought were the really great Chief Executives. Although the powerful House Speaker's extremely modest opinion about young Kennedy in the House eventually changed to respect for Kennedy's grasp of the issues as President, Rayburn remains respectfully reserved on Kennedy. Woodrow Wilson receives an accolade for intellect and Franklin D. Roosevelt for being one of the world's greatest politicians and leaders. Lyndon Johnson was Rayburn's candidate for Kennedy's job, and Rayburn's continuing reserve toward the young President reflects a widespread condition in Congress against which Kennedy continually had to struggle.

Shannon, William V., "The Kennedy Administration: The Early Months," *American Scholar*, Autumn, 1961, pp. 481–88.

Not to be judged solely from this article, but also from the columns he wrote for the *New York Post* in 1961–1962, William Shannon was the soundest observer who wrote at close hand of the Kennedy Administration. In this article, Shannon, now an editor at the *New York Times*, caught most clearly what a perceptive visitor to the White House might sense very strongly, but not often read about—that the main ideological content of the Administration was Kennedy himself and the intense loyalty of his aides was to him, personally, and to his political success. Shannon states that the so-called Irish Mafia and Sorensen do not see Kennedy as an instrument for putting into effect a social program . . . their first criterion, sometimes their sole criterion on every important problem is, how will this help "the boss" get re-elected in 1964?

He notes the "cult of toughness" which was encouraged early in the Administration, noting "there has been no fundamental re-examination of the leading ideas in any major area." The approach to the Cold War with the Soviet Union was the same as that of George F. Kennan and Dean Acheson of the 1940's and 1950's. Kennedy and his advisers did "not think the basic issues of the Cold War are negotiable" . . . and therefore "they have not moved American policy toward agreements or spheres of interest or neutralized zones in Eastern Europe or Asia." Shannon's evaluation covers less than Kennedy's first year in office, but it undoubtedly remains valid for many months afterwards. Whether Kennedy's American University speech shortly before his death marked a genuine new departure is one of the intriguing questions of the Kennedy literature.

Kazin, Alfred. "The President and Other Intellectuals," *American Scholar,* Autumn, 1961, pp. 498–516.

This rambling, rather fuzzy essay ill serves the intellectuals who had serious and specific reservations about Kennedy's performance as President. Kazin gives Kennedy credit for "freedom from the conventional prejudices," and concedes that he possesses traits of the intellectual. However, Kazin complains that Kennedy is trying to create an image of himself cultivating these traits. Kazin denies the argument put forth by Kennedy intimates that the President was undergoing enormous growth and development. "His most essential quality," Kazin concludes, "is that of the man who is always remaking himself. He is the final product of a fanatical job of self remaking."

When Kennedy found out that Kazin was planning a critical article about him, he had Schlesinger, his manager of the intellectuals' team, arrange a luncheon for the three of them. At this meal, Kennedy was both courteous and charming toward Kazin. According to Schlesinger, Kennedy remarked after the needling article appeared: "We wined and dined him, and later I told Jackie what a good time she missed, and then he went away and wrote that piece."

See also, Harris, Seymour, "Kennedy as Target; Kennedy and the Intellectuals," *New Republic,* June 1, 1963, pp. 3 ff.

Burns, James MacGregor, "The Four Kennedys of the First Year," *New York Times Magazine,* **January 14, 1962, pp. 9 f.**

Kennedy's best biographer, who had the greatest access to the facts of his life and who was much too critically objective in his biography to suit John Kennedy, here makes a cool assessment of Kennedy's first year. Professor Burns seems to have found little to overcome his previous reservations, despite his continuing affection for the man and appreciation for the difficulties of his office. Burns notes that intellectuals charge that Kennedy in power for a year still "lacks a central purpose of vision or grand design" and seems to fit well into this "managerial age of empty rhetoric and manipulation." From a recent interview with Kennedy he offers the President's explanation that he *must* act cautiously because there is lacking the condition of national emergency which made it possible for Franklin Roosevelt to act boldly and which would make it possible for Kennedy to do likewise. Of the four Kennedys mentioned in this rather gimmicky title to the article, political scientist Burns characterized the first as a Kennedy surprisingly preoccupied with foreign affairs, a second as a policy liberal having difficulties with a Congress overweighted with conservatives, and a third Kennedy as a fiscal moderate. To the great chagrin of Burns, who is the chief intellectual spokesman in America for institutional reforms in Congress and the U.S. political structure, Burns had to rank Kennedy as conservative regarding organization and institutions. Burns has hopes for a more productive second Kennedy Administration, but seems rather lukewarm about it—he closes by saying of Kennedy, "He has begun."

A truly bold move by Kennedy would have been to use his influence to have Burns, a Williams College, Massachusetts, professor, appointed to fill out Kennedy's own term in the Senate. While agreeing not to run in the next Senatorial election, Burns would then have been free to lecture the Senate on organizational reform from its own chamber. Burns was reportedly among those considered, but Kennedy instead had his seat given to a former roommate, perhaps the emptiest appointment of the entire Kennedy Administration.

Nixon, Richard Milhouse. *Six Crises.* New York: Doubleday, 1962. 460 pp.

It is interesting to know how a contender's opponent viewed his campaign. Nixon's sixth crisis, from which he never recovered, was the campaign of 1960, to which he devotes well over two hundred pages. His report is not all sour grapes by any means—his complaint of the bandwagon effect created by exaggerated reports of the Kennedy groundswell by many reporters and some pollsters (Samuel Lubell is singled out) is impressive. Nixon's criticisms will also help fair-minded Kennedy partisans to see that what they viewed as aggressive leadership by Kennedy regarding his charges of Republican negligence in Cuba and his bewailing the so-called missile and economic gaps, could be interpreted as incredible opportunism by the opposing camp. Essentially Nixon here tries to spell out the angered Eisenhower's 1960 charges against Kennedy, "juggling of promises by the inexperienced, the appeal to immediate gain and selfishness, the distortion of facts, the quick changes from fantastic charge to covert retreat . . ." Unfortunately, Kennedy readers do not read the Nixon and Eisenhower literature (and vice versa), when they might learn more from doing so than by reading any other source.

Nixon explained the origin of his book:

> When I told [Kennedy] I was considering the possibility of joining the "literary ranks" of which he is himself so distinguished a member, he expressed the thought that every public man should write a book at some time in his life, both for mental discipline and because it tends to elevate him in popular esteem to the respected status of an "intellectual."

Who was having fun with whom, the reader must decide. Ironically, though his book deserved a better fate, Nixon's *Six Crises* tended to diminish his standing with intellectuals.

Kluckhohn, Frank L. *America Listen! An Up to the Minute Report on the Chaos in Today's Washington. The Fumblings of the Kennedy Administration, The Search for Power, The Wielding of Influence Over Business and the Press.* Paperback, Derby,

Connecticut: Monarch Books, Inc., 1963. 315 pp. New enlarged edition.

The Minute Man breathlessness of the title is indicative; Kluckhohn is a tireless warner against what he considers the ever-spreading Communist menace to the world. He worked from 1956 to 1961 in the U.S. Bureau of Security and Consular Affairs, which must be to the right wing what the Farm Security Administration once was to the left. For the most part the book expresses the standard ultra-conservative alarm that the battle against Communism and domestic statism is being hampered while the true story of these occurrences is being withheld from the public.

Although some of Kluckhohn's sections stop just short of accusing Kennedy of fluoridation of the drinking water, there are many sections that are carefully reasoned. The real contribution the book makes for any reader, whether or not he shares the author's right-wing bias, is to show how the Kennedy Administration's news management looked to one of strongly conservative, but not fringe group, persuasion.

Rukeyser, Merryle Stanley. *The Kennedy Recession.* Paperback, Derby, Connecticut: Monarch Books, Inc., 1963. 220 pp.

Many of the writers about Kennedy and the economy are of a modern liberal persuasion—Galbraith, Seymour Harris, Hobart Rowen, among them. Here a conservative newspaper economic analyst and business consultant argues that Kennedy is trying to overmanage the economy and "repeal the law of supply and demand," and he is even doing these things in a botched-up way. There is a nostalgic air about the writing, which, nevertheless, truly captures how many of Rukeyser's clients and readers looked at the Kennedy Administration.

Krock, Arthur. "Kennedy at 46," *The New York Times,* June 2, 1963, Section E, p. 11.

The New York Times' old Washington hand, who long knew the Kennedy family, titled Kennedy's first book, as well as the Richard Whalen book about Kennedy's father, and helped Mrs. Jacqueline Kennedy get her job as a reporter, here pays a birthday tribute to the President, saying he had exceeded even the high promise of his youth. "There is, however, one defect in his Presidency for which long personal acquaintance with him and his political principles left one unprepared. This is his failure to follow through acts and policies firmly undertaken." He cites some tough lines on foreign policy from *Why England Slept,* for which book Krock had helped Kennedy obtain the Pulitzer Prize. Unfortunately, the only example of Kennedy's failure to follow through which Krock cites is his failure to defeat Cuba; this places the piece in the category of an informed and interesting right-wing critique.

Krock went further in an interview with William Manchester early during the Kennedy Administration, in which he remarked that the President "has repeated every one of the errors of weaknesses he attributed to Eisenhower. . . . I'm doubtful we did the best we could in selecting this President." To date, Krock has not fully revealed his evaluation of Kennedy's entire tenure.

Burns, James MacGregor, "The Legacy of the 1,000 Days," *New York Times Magazine,* December 1, 1963, pp. 27 ff.

Kennedy's chief biographer here notes that the late President's admirable personal qualities will assure him a place in history. The date of the piece suggests the emotions which Burns must have felt for his friend, but the biographer remained true to the objectivity which Kennedy admired, even though it sometimes rankled the President. Burns goes slightly further in testifying to Kennedy's commitment than he did in his resume of Kennedy's first year in office, but he still makes a distinction between commitment of intellect and commitment of heart. The latter, to Burns, is a necessary ingredient of leadership which can achieve greatness. "I believe he did make a complete political and intellectual commitment to his policies and programs. It will never be known whether he ultimately would have made a commitment of the heart." When a reader's letter asked Burns why most people were on the verge of tears after the assassination if Kennedy had no heart, Burns sadly replied,

> I define commitment of the heart in a rather special way: a willingness to take extreme political risks on behalf of some goal—much as did the heroes of *Profiles in Courage.* I don't believe President Kennedy wanted to make that kind of commitment: perhaps this made him a more effective "practical politician." (*ibid.* December 15, 1963, p. 4.)

Lasky, Victor. *JFK: The Man and the Myth.* New York: Macmillan, 1963. 653 pp.

This book grew out of a seventy-five-page work by the same author entitled *John F. Kennedy: What's Behind the Image?* Washington, D.C.: Free World Press, Inc., 1960. Lasky, a right-wing journalist and controversialist, opens *What's Behind the Image?* with a long quotation critical of Kennedy from the liberal *Nation,* and proceeds to quote whatever else can be found to discredit Kennedy. They are culled from sources ranging indiscriminately from leftish I. F. Stone to the right-wing *National Review,* and are used to prove alternately that Kennedy is power mad and a weakling, an arch manipulator and an incompetent. As Lasky's file became enlarged by more and more attacks on Kennedy from all sources, the original *John F. Kennedy: What's Behind the Image?* seems to have expanded into the large: *JFK: The Man and the Myth.*

Like the earlier work from which it sprang, *JFK: The Man and the Myth* is in the assault tradition of John T. Flynn; it shows a conclusion firmly held before the gathering of evidence began. Unfortunately, the evidence offered does not show original research, extensive interviewing, or careful analysis of implications. The book suffers from a jumble of contradictory critiques, sometimes at the expense of a sustained central argument.

Nevertheless, the book and, more importantly, the sources cited, provide a useful series of hypotheses which run counter to those in the major biographies. Some of them, particularly those dealing with Kennedy's attempt at generating a desired image and the contradictions within the Kennedy political coalition, are well worth testing out in a more serious way than Lasky's method achieved.

A month after Kennedy's assassination his *Profiles in Courage* had become the best selling general book throughout the country. But, interestingly, a *New York Times* inquiry in Dallas at that time showed Lasky's *JFK: The Man and the Myth* to be that city's best-selling general book. (*New York Times,* December 29, 1963).

Mailer, Norman. *The Presidential Papers.* New York: Putnam, 1963. 310 pp. Paperback ed., New York: Bantam Books, 1964. 310 pp.

The pieces in this collection were dismissed by some readers as another edition of *Advertisements for Myself*. However, although only a small part is of lasting general interest, here is a highly individual opinion by a novelist and cultural commentator who shows some insight. The book also contains the most stinging rebuke Kennedy ever received. Arthur Schlesinger gave Mailer's work a serious reading and the more imaginative reader of the Kennedy literature may wish to, also. Mailer, who had met Kennedy a few times, became caught in a Kennedy mystique of his own making at the Democratic convention in Los Angeles in 1960. Kennedy for him became a mysterious figure with the "wisdom of a man who senses death within him and gambles that he can cure it by risking his life." Greatly interested in violence himself, Mailer associated Kennedy with the possibility of violence and unexpected happenings. "With such a man in office," he wrote, "the myth of the nation would again be engaged, and the fact that he was a Catholic would shiver a first existential vibration of consciousness into the mind of the white Protestants." When showed this piece, Kennedy commented noncommitally, "It really runs on, doesn't it?" The main argument of the collection is waged among Kennedy, Mailer, and Fidel Castro, to whom Mailer has signed his very public letter, "Still Your Brother." At first he urges Castro to make an accommodation with Kennedy who, Mailer states, "wishes to be considered a great man in the cultivated verdict of history." But after the disastrous military assault on Castro's Cuba, Mailer makes his most trenchant and valid criticism of Kennedy. "You are a virtuoso in political management," he jibes, "but you will never understand the revolutionary passion" which moves the poor and the alienated. "Do you propose," Mailer writes to Kennedy, "to get around that by putting higher I.Q.'s into the seersuckers of the Central Intelligence Agency?" Kennedy's once fervent followers have now left him because they "now fear you are not deep enough to direct the destinies of our lives." But Mailer's most taunting remark was to sneeringly remind Kennedy that Castro was "one of the great figures of the twentieth century, at the present moment a far greater figure than yourself."

Neustadt, Richard E., "Kennedy in the Presidency: A Premature Appraisal," *Political Science Quarterly,* September, 1964, pp. 321–34.

The author of *Presidential Power,* and an ardent admirer and adviser of President Kennedy, establishes the main criteria by which he believes a President should be judged, and, with considerable objectivity measures the Kennedy performance accordingly. He highly approves of Kennedy's understanding of the Presidency, his "feel" for the exercise of power, and his judgment about priorities. An important if preliminary evaluation by a scholar well grounded in the standards of political science as well as the daily strains of the Executive Office of the President. Neustadt's main weakness is his failure to understand what the Eisenhower Administration was all about and why the Kennedy and Eisenhower Administrations were so much alike.

Hagan, Roger. "Between Two Eras," *The Correspondent*, January–February 1964, pp. 33–42.

If Lyndon Johnson had read the Kennedy literature, he would have sensed earlier that the intellectuals can no longer be counted upon in the conventional Cold War. As in the case of other thoughtful pieces cited in this bibliography, Roger Hagan, an editor on this exciting journal of advanced intellectual thinking, finds Kennedy's greatest failure in his inability to move beyond a bipolar Cold War between America and Russia. Hagan admits that the 1960's demand a policy largely incompatible with recent American tradition, and that whenever Kennedy ventured upon it, he got into trouble at home. He admits that "there were hints of an alternative vision, of two systems evolving with mutual borrowing . . . and jointly exercising a restraining and guiding hand on the more impetuous new societies." But more clearly than any other writer, Hagan explains how Kennedy was trapped in his vision of opposed systems in deadly embrace, in an historic trial in which the "tough" society survives and the "soft" one succumbs. (See also, Kennedy's *Why England Slept*.) Hagan admits that this vision is a favorite of thoughtful and educated people. "With all this caution, there were kinds of ideas to which John Kennedy was particularly vulnerable, schemes whose short-term promise obscured to him their long term insidious qualities." Military aid and the para-military and counter-insurgency enthusiasms of certain of his associates are cited as examples, and Hagan might have included Kennedy's foolishness over civil defense, the consequences of which he came to regret. Such enthusiasm got him into trouble later as it did in Cuba and was doing in Vietnam, and Kennedy, Hagan tells us, "had to wait, and perhaps hope for disasters to discredit them."

Despite these errors of judgment, Hagan pays Kennedy great credit for a will and ambition which routed us towards a liberal path — largely by playing skillfully on America's guilt about backsliding.

> It seemed to be Kennedy's hope to join Jefferson, Lincoln, and Wilson in being one of those semi-centennial leaders who recall to Americans their exemplary role in the world and revive the springs of idealism in a society that lapses easily into greed.

Hagan has less to say about domestic matters but he trenchantly asks why Kennedy couldn't deal with Congress. "Perhaps because he was decent, or young, or fair, or intellectual; perhaps because the issues were too divisive; perhaps because his team was basically incompetent." Hagan then has one of the most penetrating passages in the Kennedy literature. There was, he says,

> a deep difference between the expectations of Johnson and Kennedy about their fellow men, which may have been a key to whatever failures Kennedy experienced. Somewhere in deep, Johnson had an understanding of the mixture on which human beings run, and thus on which governments conduct their affairs; a mixture of the reasonable and the childish, the idealistic and the cynical, the dignified and the corny. John Kennedy, like most of us perusing these pages, could never cover so much ground. Even if we understood it we couldn't carry it off and neither could he.

Despite this, Hagan still bets on intelligent Presidential brain in this complicated world and warns intellectuals who were disturbed by the difficulties encountered by the Kennedy Administration not to indulge in self-depreciation and resign themselves to turning matters over entirely to the wheeler-dealers. Hagan concludes "perhaps Kennedy's monument will not be anything he did but what he seemed to be." Hagan has not undertaken to prove much of what he has written, but few pieces provide as many hypotheses from which serious research may begin, research which might either prove, disprove, or modify the preliminary conclusions he has boldly set out for us.

Carleton, William Graves, "Kennedy in History: An Early Appraisal," *Antioch Review*, Fall, 1964, pp. 277-99.

While to some scholars it may seem rather early to begin serious evaluations of Kennedy, evaluation will not be any easier later on, Professor Carleton warns us, and deferred conclusions will be as controversial as current ones. This historian-political scientist's qualifications for appraisal are that he is a penetrating and scholarly writer about both American domestic and foreign policy, and also one of the shrewdest judges now writing about political institutions and political character—the reaction of men to their office. On the positive side, Carleton notes that "no Administration in history staffed the executive departments with as many competent, dedicated and brilliant men." He thoroughly approves of the way Kennedy widened and intellectualized the FDR brain trust concept. But this machinery produced only modest results and Carleton seriously doubts, on historical grounds, whether a second term would have found the President more powerful than he was in the first. Here Carleton and history may have proved a poor guide, especially if Barry Goldwater had run against Kennedy, as Kennedy believed likely, and insured a Democratic Congressional landslide.

Carleton (himself once an Al Smith man, and who has written elsewhere about anti-Catholic prejudice) found in his tours during the Kennedy campaign that "In Protestant areas citizens were made to feel like bigots if they voted against Kennedy," a conclusion confirmed by Theodore White. Kennedy's Democrats, Carleton claims, used this theme effectively. He repeats the claim, more fully developed in his *Harper's Magazine* article cited elsewhere in this bibliography, that Kennedy unfortunately contributed to a "personalized, plebiscite" Presidency, a serious charge worthy of careful examination.

Because Carleton is not as emotionally committed to the Cold War as most of the writers of the Kennedy literature, he is free to make important points of criticism on foreign policy which most other writers shy away from, and which many others utter only in private. Carleton recognized that an age of multilateral diplomacy was opening up and Kennedy, for all his sophisticated speeches, did not know what to do about it. Carleton writes of the "alarmist flavor" of the 1960 campaign, a fact which is seldom examined seriously by other writers on Kennedy. More controversial, but demanding serious consideration, is Carleton's estimate that in his first two years Kennedy "needlessly fanned the flames of the Cold War"; his alarmist Inaugural Address was "already historically off-key, more suited to the Stalinist era than 1961," and his first Message to Congress was even more alarmist. In Carleton's opinion Kennedy also over-reacted to Khrushchev on the Berlin question. Carleton gives Kennedy credit for greatly bolstering the country's military establishment but does not find how this was used constructively for diplomatic initiatives.

While these viewpoints may seem startling to many Americans, they are not uncommon among serious intellectuals here and abroad. To these critics, Carleton's interpretations are, then, not as controversial as they might appear. There is, however, a definitely arguable conclusion: "People of our prosaic era are yearning for a romantic hero, as the James Dean cult among our youth revealed. Now they have one."

Fairlie, Henry. "He Was a Man of Only One Season," *New York Times Magazine,* November, 1965, pp. 28 f.

The author, a British political writer frequently appearing in *The Spectator,* delivers one long yawn of boredom at the entire Kennedy saga. It is admittedly a subjective view, and therefore individually valuable, but Fairlie's claim that his view is widely shared in Europe requires more evidence. He states that it is possible that Kennedy is ill served by his biographers but that it is quite possible that his (Fairlie's) boredom with the Sorensen book stems from a basic boredom with the man Kennedy. In Sorensen's book, he states, it was as if there were no deep questions about Kennedy to be asked and therefore none to be answered. After all, Fairlie states, a wry and cool way of looking at things isn't enough to sustain interest for hundreds of pages. If Kennedy was praised as so disciplined, "what was in him that required such discipline?" To author Fairlie, Kennedy's vision of politics was almost entirely one of method; at the end of eighteen months in office there was still no clear sense of direction. Kennedy was particularly ineffective in questions of political economy and little understood the Negro question. "One can scan his actions and his speeches," Fairlie concludes, "and find no profound concept of the nature of politics, of the character of his country or his countrymen, or of the moral crisis of his age." This is an interesting alternative view of the man, but one which unfortunately rests largely on assertion.

"The Kennedy Legend and the Johnson Performance," *Time,* November 26, 1965.

One of the articles which maintains that the enormous esteem still held for Kennedy and his manner of doing things tends to overshadow the very solid domestic accomplishments of his successor.

Muggeridge, Malcolm, "Books," *Esquire,* December, 1965. pp. 118 f.

The subject of Kennedy so annoyed this English humorist and critical essayist that it continually drove him across that important line which divides the splendid mocker from the smart aleck. Muggeridge's view of Kennedy is as well set out in this *Esquire* book review of Sorensen's *Kennedy* as anywhere, but those who can obtain it may wish to read Muggeridge's "Kennedy the Man and Myth," *Maclean's* Magazine (a Canadian monthly), April, 1966, pp. 14–15.

Muggeridge sees Kennedy as the complete staff product—when Sorensen praises Kennedy's work he is actually praising himself, and there is no Kennedy joke which we can be certain did not come out of the campaign file marked "humor"; in fact, Muggeridge retorts that we cannot be certain anything Kennedy ever said was his own—a claim readers will have to test against their memories of the televised press conferences. Muggeridge does not believe, as does Victor Lasky apparently, that Kennedy was a bad man; he sees him rather as a sleepwalker.

Lippman, Walter. *Conversations with Walter Lippman.* Transcribed with the Cooperation of the Columbia Broadcasting System. Introduction by Edward Weeks. Boston: Little, Brown, 1965. 242 pp.

This wise essayist shared Kennedy's disappointment about the gap between his aspirations and his accomplishments. Not as an apologist but as an astute analyst, Lippman explains the domestic and foreign circumstances which defeated many of Kennedy's aims.

CRITICS: GENTLE AND SEVERE 141

Bailey, T. A. "Johnson and Kennedy: The Two Thousand Days," *New York Times Magazine,* November 6, 1966, pp. 30 ff.

In a dispassionate manner the author Bailey points out how much more Johnson had to show for his thousand days than Kennedy could claim. For discussion of this see succeeding issues of November 28, 1966, pp. 159–60, and December 4, 1966, p. 22.

Lippman, Walter, "The Legend Reappraised," *New York Post,* November 22, 1967.

The most respected American political analyst here attempts an assessment of Kennedy three years after his death. Lippman had been greatly attracted to Kennedy personally, especially to his spirit and intentions, but his scarcely concealed disappointment in President Kennedy's actions and achievements injected an element of embarrassment into his writing about Kennedy. A usually consistent pleader for realism and rationality, Lippman finds he can approve of the legendary image of Kennedy which is being built with such artistry. He acknowledges the legend contains only part of the truth—that the record of the Kennedy Administration is a "mixed collection of errors and false starts and brilliant illuminations of the future." In foreign affairs Kennedy fumbled in his early dealings with Europe, at the Bay of Pigs in Cuba and in his early dealings with Khrushchev, but he was masterly in his handling of the Cuban missile crisis and in using the advantages which flowed from this to mark the beginning of the end of the Cold War. On the domestic front he notes his deadlock with Congress on the negative side, but credits him with being the first President to adopt the teachings of modern economics. "It would be hard to put together an imposing record of what he actually accomplished here, but there is the undeniable fact that a whole generation of thinkers and experts in these matters was inspired by him and swear by him now," Lippman concludes. He explains this phenomenon as resulting from Kennedy's ability to make people believe they could fashion the means of controlling their own destinies even in a threatening and confusing age.

Lippman is one of the most cogent and graceful writers on public affairs of any era and this is one of the most important brief pieces written by those in sympathy with the continuing Kennedy legend.

CHAPTER VIII.

The Assassination: The Warren Commission, Doubts, and Alternative Explanations

THE ASSASSINATION

The Torch is Passed: The Associated Press Story of the Death of a President. Edited by the Editors of the Associated Press. New York: Associated Press, 1963. 93 pp.

This book is a memorial by the reporters who recorded the President's death in Dallas. It sold more than 4,000,000 copies and provided many readers with the main written version of what occurred. A compilation with similar impact was *Four Days: The Historical Record of the Death of President Kennedy.* Compiled by United Press International and American Heritage Publishing Co. New York: American Heritage Pub. Co., 1964. 143 pp. Illustrated. The most detailed account of the Dallas tragedy is to be found, of course, in *The Warren Commission Report* and *The Witnesses,* cited below.

Hughes, Emmet John, "An Echo in Silence," *Newsweek,* December 2, 1963, p. 52.

America's most eloquent writer of political prose pays tribute to that quality of facing hard and lonely decisions which Hughes believes made Kennedy an outstanding leader. Hughes summarizes a mood which was widely felt at the time the piece was published when he quotes Henry David Thoreau's paean to a short life: "Let its report be short and round like a rifle, so that it may hear its own echo in the surrounding silence."

Bradlee, Benjamin. *That Special Grace.* Philadelphia: Lippincott, 1964. Unpaged.

   The original version of a friend's appreciation of President Kennedy's style and personality can be found in the magazine for which he was a White House correspondent, *Newsweek,* December 2, 1963, which issue also contains a dignified account of the assassination and the immediate consequences.

Dunning, John L., "The Kennedy Assassination as Viewed by the Communist Media," *Journalism Quarterly,* Spring, 1964, pp. 163–69.

   This roundup indicates that, with the major exception of China, the Communist press treated the President's death in good taste, even though analysis of the assassination was made to fit the official Communist line. Indeed, the Communists expressed far fewer doubts of our official version of the assassination than were revealed by other surveys in noncommunist Europe and Asia.

Manchester, William. *The Death of a President.* New York: Harper & Row, 1967. 710 pp.

   Even before the controversy and personal drama provoked by this book, the Kennedy literature had already generated some of the most celebrated literary controversies of recent years. Hot interest in its details ranged from the Algonquin Bar to the readers of *Film Secrets.*

   The legal and personal controversy threatening publication of the book was, it turned out, more important to its publicity than its ultimate content. Because writer Manchester, in return for extraordinary Kennedy family cooperation in research and interviewing for the book, signed a specific agreement to submit the manuscript for approval of President Kennedy's widow and brother Robert, he was induced to delete passages amounting to reportedly more than a thousand words. Most of the book's supposedly "juicier" deletions found their way into news magazine reports of the controversy, and they do not indicate that much of importance was lost, however reprehensible the repression may be judged to be.

The contributions of this gracefully written book are many. First, its thoroughness in tracing the four days associated with the President's death helps dispel many unsupportable rumors. Although creditable as this is, Manchester does not exhibit the kind of skeptically analytical mind which would find it comfortable fundamentally to question an established version of a crucial event. The next contribution of the book is bringing to partial public view the emotional conflicts between the Johnson supporters and the Kennedy group in and returning from Dallas which were so politically important, even though glossed over by most writers for the sake of national and party harmony.

If read with proper perspective, *The Death of a President* also helps illuminate the quarrel—however unfair and irrational it may be —which important segments of America have with Texas and things Texan. Politics is carried on only in part by forces rational in nature. This book, beset by critics on all sides, was denounced by Johnson partisans partly because it brought into the open the strained relations between President Johnson and Robert Kennedy and some other Kennedy staff members during the first days of the Administration of John Kennedy's successor. Johnson partisans and objective observers are justified in complaining that the story surrounding the changing of the guard told here is told largely through the eyes of the Kennedy family and Kennedy partisans. Manchester is particularly inclined to accept uncritically the sentimental recollections of President Kennedy's widow regarding events and impressions before and after the assassination.

Nevertheless, what Manchester communicates about differing Johnson-Kennedy perceptions is important to an understanding of the politics of the period. Elements only partially rational—including personal distastes, conflicting legends, vague longings for a "restoration" of a past dream—currently play so large a part in American political life that the more prosaic news analyst scarcely knows how to deal with them. The refusal of President Kennedy's widow ever to visit the White House under President Johnson's tenure, for example, created an uneasiness in political life which was seldom mentioned, was not measurable, but was ever present. Manchester suggests the roots of this expression through declination.

Manchester is certainly no prosaic writer. He has a useful sense of romance and the role of the irrational. Sometimes he carries it too far as in the eerie quality he achieves by using code name chapter headings such as "Lancer," "Charcoal," "Wand" and "Castle." His excessive identification with the person of President Kennedy adds to the drama but detracts from the perspective of the overly long and detailed book.

Manchester lets himself go completely in indulging in a favorite American pastime of psychoanalyzing Oswald. His attempt to impose motivation upon Oswald—something the Warren Commission sagely refrained from doing—is ludicrous. Oswald is pictured as turning in frustration from his wife to the solace of TV. Manchester writes: "Apparently he was intent upon the flickering screen. In fact, he was going mad."

Corry, John. *The Manchester Affair.* New York: Putnam, 1967. 223 pp.

Readers who want the details of a classic case of public bad manners can save themselves much time by reading this small book by the writer assigned by the *New York Times* to report the case. There are also books on the subject by Lawrence Van Gelder and Arnold Bennet, as well as incredibly detailed running accounts in newspapers and news magazines, but Corry seems to know the story as well as any. In the style of his employer he understates some bizarre episodes, but he has a few firm conclusions. The Kennedys, Corry states, "are really not very good in dealing with people who have other commitments; they are, in fact vulnerable to them." Despite the fact that Mrs. Kennedy emerges from this book as a youthful eccentric, Corry concluded:

> It was really a mistake for either one of them [Jacqueline or Robert Kennedy] to have got mixed up with Bill Manchester, his was a style entirely different from theirs, far too exotic for them, and when they could not direct him, they began to fight him. It was sad all around.

Epstein, Edward J. "Manchester Unexpurgated: From 'Death of Lancer' to 'Death of a President.' " *Commentary,* July, 1967, pp. 25–32.

The author of *Inquest* here presents what he flatly states is the essence of a romantic first version of Manchester's *Death of a President.* Citing direct quotes Epstein indicates that Manchester originally contemplated a version of the story in which John Kennedy was even more a legendary hero and Lyndon Johnson and Texas politicians even greater villains than in the final version of the work. Epstein here violates a rather long standing rule of fairness that at the time an author publishes a work he is entitled to be judged publicly upon what he agreed to publish, not upon some real or alleged preliminary version.

The more sensational lines deleted from the final Manchester manuscript upon demand of the Kennedy family appeared in the leading news magazines during the period of the legal controversy over publication and serialization of the book. It is anticipated that in due time versions of the original manuscript pirated abroad will enter the United States, but perhaps only after public interest has waned.

Such was the aura of weirdness surrounding the controversy that many persons believed and gave word of mouth dissemination to a most preposterous bad taste spoof of the affair by Paul Krassner, "The Parts that Were Left Out of the Kennedy Book" in #74, 1967 edition of *The Realist.* Despite the fact that his piece appalled even admirers of black humor, and the fact that Krassner publicly laughed at those taken in by his squalid joke, even this version continues to live and spread.

THE WARREN COMMISSION

Report of the Warren Commission on the Assassination of President Kennedy: The Dramatic Official Answer to Who Killed Kennedy. Introduction by Harrison E. Salisbury, and Other Material Prepared by the *New York Times.* Paperback ed., New York: Bantam Books, Inc., Copyright 1963, 1964 by the New York Times Company. 726 pp. Hardcover ed., New York: McGraw-Hill Book Company, 1964. 800 pp.

This work is not only dramatic, as its subtitle indicates, it also reads like a fairy story. I say fairy story, because a novel would require more underlying credibility. The report rests upon amazing coincidences and unlikely (though not impossible) sequences of events which strain the most vivid imagination. There are the murky worlds of Soviet and American intelligence agencies, the American underworld, and the

Cuban Embassy. There are extraordinary human error and sublime innocence. There are false witnesses and vacillating witnesses, who either change their stories or deny giving them in order to coincide with the official version of events. Flagrant news leaks have all the earmarks of the government's attempt to create a prejudgment. Finally, the Chief Justice who lent his name to the Commission asks the public to have reservations about its findings, then asks us not to. And, haunting the entire report is the greatest weakness of the case: the alleged assassin's clear lack of motive.

All this is not to say the *Report* is false, or not the best we could expect under exceedingly difficult circumstances. But it is to say that people will continue to read the *Report* with a skeptical eye until further information appears to answer doubts.

The paperback edition contains all the published *Report* of the President's Commission on the Assassination of President Kennedy, commonly known as the *Warren Commission Report,* including every illustration and exhibit in the U.S. Government Printing Office Edition of the official report. It does not include the internal memoranda of the Commission (not yet declassified) and such other material as the Commission may keep classified for security reasons or reasons of taste. Since much controversy has raged around the autopsy reports, it should be noted that Commander James J. Humes in his autopsy report from Bethesda Naval Hospital, stated: "Black-and-white and color photographs depicting significant findings are exposed but not developed. These photographs were placed in the custody of Agent Roy H. Kellerman of the U.S. Secret Service, who executed a receipt therefore."

Kellerman had ridden in the front seat of Kennedy's ill-fated car in Dallas, and was in charge of President Kennedy's trip to Texas. These photographs have not been made available to researchers. *The New York Times,* December 17, 1964, also reported that the brief, fragmentary pencil notes made by the doctors at the Bethesda Hospital were thrown away when the typewritten reports were prepared.

For reasons which have not been adequately explained, Oswald's twelve hours of questioning by Dallas, F.B.I., and Secret Service officials were not recorded stenographically or on tape. The Commission committed its working papers to the National Archives, "where they can be permanently preserved under the rules and regulations of the

National Archives and Federal Law." From time to time additional memoranda is declassified and made available to researchers. The most recent declassified material in the National Archives (Used by Epstein in his book *Inquest*) is an FBI "Summary Report" of January 13, 1964, which, contrary to Humes's autopsy report of a neck exit wound, states that the bullet which penetrated the President's back "penetrated less than a finger-length."

There will be requests for further data. Unquestionably an almost unprecedented amount of material is already available, and an enormous number of rumors painstakingly checked out, so that one must have some sympathy with the Commission's staff members who became testy when challenged.

This volume begins with "A Prologue: Death in Dallas," written —in Dallas—by *New York Times* correspondent Tom Wicker on the day of Kennedy's assassination, November 22, 1963. Wicker's piece, which was gracefully written under tremendous pressure, contains this statement: "Dr. Malcolm Perry, an attending surgeon, and Dr. Kemp Clark, chief of neurosurgery at the Parkland Hospital, gave more details. Mr. Kennedy was hit by a bullet in the throat, just below the Adam's apple, they said. This wound had the appearance of a bullet's entry." Numerous persons have preferred to believe this first doctor's report, which raises serious doubts of the President having been shot only from behind, rather than believe the later autopsy report from Bethesda Naval Hospital. This prologue is followed by an introduction by Harrison Salisbury, Assistant Managing Editor of *The New York Times*. Salisbury's tone is hostile toward those who would continue to ask questions. He is repelled by those who believe that the weight and authority of the American Establishment—Government, Big Business, and the Power Structure of Society—have been behind a concerted move to establish a single man theory. Some of the Commission's critics, such as attorney Mark Lane, and writers Leo Sauvage, Thomas C. Buchanan, and Joachim Joesten, he attempts to refute specifically. Against others he makes more general charges. While he does not denounce all skepticism, Salisbury states that

> frequently these theories were self-serving—designed to advance some special political goal or cause. Some have had the objective of undermining the standing of the United States and its government structure. Some have aimed at sowing distrust and confu-

sion at home. Others seek to convey to foreign countries the image of a violent America, helpless in the face of dangerous forces.

The Commission, he stated, had labored diligently to lay for all time "the aura of vicious and irresponsible rumor which has grown up around the Kennedy assassination."

Salisbury gives a summary of the other attempts on American Presidents' lives and repeats the often heard concept that in the American context assassins acting alone have greater credibility than in other countries where conspiracies are more common. The author then makes this extraordinary statement: "No material question now remains unresolved as far as the death of President Kennedy is concerned." He gives one reason why the *Report* may not be considered the "final word"; it is "not because the evidence is not toweringly clear," but because we all share a sense of psychological guilt for the President's death.

By summer of 1966, political analyst Richard Rovere, in an introduction to Epstein's *Inquest* (a sharp critique of the Commission), delivered a stern rebuke to Salisbury, and Elliot Fremont-Smith, who is book editor and colleague of Salisbury on *The New York Times*. Commenting on Epstein's book Rovere warned:

> If the Warren Commission's version of the assassination is correct, it is not completely faithful to the evidence—which includes unexplained contradictions and unevaluated doubts—that the Commission had available to it.

Salisbury's tone was only slightly less intimidating than that of FBI Director J. Edgar Hoover, who told the Commission

> I, personally, feel that any finding of the Commission will not be accepted by everybody, because there are bound to be some extremists who have very pronounced views without any foundation for them, who will disagree violently with whatever finding the Commission makes.

Other motives, for continued questioning were, according to Hoover, "either publicity purposes or otherwise."

After a factual summary of the *Report* by reporter Anthony Lewis, editor James Reston comments more on the drama than the substance of the *Report*. "It has provided enough material to intrigue novelists and dramatists for years to come," he writes,

> and thus it has added materially to the Kennedy legend. . . . Now the central mystery of who killed the President has been answered by the Commission only in the process of raising a new catalogue of mysteries. Now the main characters in the play have been surrounded by a host of new characters, each of whom appears briefly at a critical moment with some vital testimony, only to disappear without our knowing much about who they are.

He concludes almost despairingly, "The whole story is not only beyond the journalist, but beyond most historians as well."

A Foreword by the Commission itself then establishes its powers and functions, the nature of the hearings (which were closed to the public unless the interviewee requested otherwise), and the reasons the Commission proceeded in the way it did. The Commission points out that it was not a court presiding over an adversary proceeding, which means that no one would have the primary job of cross-examining in the interests of the defendant, Lee Harvey Oswald. However, in an apparent concession that some kind of check on the Commission's fairness, and from outside the Commission's formal framework, might be appropriate, the Commission had President Walter E. Craig of the American Bar Association and his appointed assistants participate in the investigation, with the right of questioning witnesses and "to advise the Commission whether in his opinion the proceedings conformed to the basic principles of American justice." The problem here was that, whatever its intention, the Commission's report was treated in many quarters as a court which had found the undefended Oswald solely guilty.

Many doubters could not fail to note that of the six members appointed to the Committee by President Johnson, one was a former head of the Central Intelligence Agency and another was Senator Richard B. Russell, who was the main champion of the CIA in Congress. Critics from the right complained that the Commission was headed by a Chief Justice who was undergoing attacks (largely by themselves) for his allegedly "liberal" Supreme Court opinions. Critics from the left noted that the composition of the Commission showed a conservative, or at least an Establishment, bias. Observers of the center thought the Commission prestigious, and unobjectionable within the framework of American politics. One professor of public law, however, Robert E. Cushman, posed a thoughtful challenge to the Commission's constitutionality, in the *New York University Law Review*.

A problem which proved impossible for the Commission to deal with satisfactorily was the use of federal investigative agencies to investigate a case in which their own conduct had been brought into question. The FBI had prepared a preliminary report on the assassination, which, by December, 1963, had already leaked to the press and resulted in headlines which indicated the Government's view that Oswald, a loner, had been responsible for the assassination. FBI Director Hoover had agreed to the withholding of this report because, as he told the Commission, "I feel that the report of any agency of Government investigating what might be some shortcomings on the part of any other agencies of Government ought to be reviewed by an impartial group as this Commission."

At the same time, however, the Commission could hardly set up its own FBI. The Commissioner's Foreword explains this awkward problem in this manner:

> Because of the diligence, the cooperation, and the facilities of the Federal investigative agencies, it was unnecessary for the Commission to employ investigators other than the members of the Commission's legal staff.

But, it continues,

> the Commission recognized, however, that special measures were required whenever the facts or rumors called for an appraisal of the agencies themselves. The staff reviewed in detail the actions of several agencies, particularly the Federal Bureau of Investigation, the Secret Service, the Central Intelligence Agency, and the Department of State. . . . In some instances the members of the Commission also reviewed the files [of these agencies] in person.

The reader will simply have to take the Commission's word that it had complete access to these files because on this point, in contrast to most of the Commission's testimony, there is no way of cross-checking. The FBI conducted an impressive 25,000 interviews and re-interviews for the Commission, and the Secret Service 1,550, with the CIA, the Defense Intelligence Agencies, and other Federal and local investigative agencies also lending their help. Yet there is much evidence in the Warren Commission material to undermine confidence in the efficiency and reliability of the intelligence agencies.

The first chapter of the lengthy report runs forty-seven pages and provides a concise summary of events, followed by the Commission's conclusions and recommendations. Later chapters treat in a detailed way the assassination, the assassin, his detention and murder, and his possible motives. In keeping with its evidence, the Commission declines to specify the motive. A chapter is also devoted to the system of protecting the President.

Chapter VI, which treats (and refutes) those various versions of the assassination that involve conspiracy, should be studied carefully by any serious reader before he begins studying the books and articles which challenge the official version of the assassination. Here in this chapter, the Commission's open-mindedness in refusing to impute bad faith to doubters is a model worthy of emulation by those who write about the *Report*. The Commission, however, finds no evidence of conspiracy.

The reader doing serious research on the question will wish to examine also the 235-page appendix in the paperback volume which provides detailed ballistics and medical testimony, more biographical detail on Oswald and Jack Ruby, and a further section on "Speculation and Rumors."

For a discussion of alleged interagency arguments about which working papers of the Warren Commission should be released see: Allen, Robert S. and Scott, Paul, "Washington Report: Assassination Papers May be Made Public," *Allentown* (Pennsylvania) *Evening News Chronicle,* October 14, 1966, or other newspapers in which this column is published. An interesting report of a visit to the National Archives stacks storing the working papers of the Warren Commission is offered by Michael J. Berlin in "The Warren Report and its Critics: A New Inquiry?" *New York Post,* March 11, 1967. He states, in part, "Stacked on both sides of one long aisle, and in part of another are 900 of these file boxes—300 cubic feet—filled with 1,555 Warren Commission documents. About a third are classified."

Finally, the reader should be aware that along with this *Report,* the

Commission delivered twenty-six closely spaced volumes, fifteen of testimony and eleven of exhibits, and numbering more than 17,000 pages. This important supplement to the *Report,* officially entitled: U.S. Commission on the Assassination of President Kennedy. *Hearings.* Volume 1–15 "Hearings": Volumes 16–26 "Exhibits." Washington, D.C.: Government Printing Office, 1964, may be purchased from the Government Printing Office, but there is available a more usable, abridged form, which is discussed in the next entry.

The Witnesses: The Highlights of Hearings Before the Warren Commission On the Assassination of President Kennedy. Selected and edited by the *New York Times* for this edition. Introduction by Anthony Lewis. New York: McGraw-Hill, 1964. 634 pp. Paperback ed. (here reviewed), New York: Bantam Books, Inc., December, 1964. 626 pp.

It is not the *Warren Commission Report,* but rather this testimony of witnesses which was submitted along with the *Report,* that truly reveals what a fantastic story the Dallas tragedy was. Editors and staff members of the *New York Times* have contributed a great service in sensibly arranging and selecting some 300,000 words from the twenty-six volumes of testimony and exhibits which the Warren Commission submitted along with its *Report.* Whereas the testimony in the official document was presented in chronological order, in this edition the *Times* has arranged it (in a way similar to that of the Commission *Report*) under subject categories, e.g., Assassination, the Arrest, the Assassin's Killer, the President's Safety, etc. A sixty-four-page selection of key exhibits may be found in the middle of the book, and in the back of the book is a list of the witnesses, some of whom are not in this collection, as they appeared chronologically before the Warren Commission.

The *Times* staff seems to have made a fair selection of the testimony which forms the heart of the evidence upon which the Commission based its final conclusion; indeed, the selection is about as much as the eager general reader would wish to read. However, it is important not to draw improper conclusions from the selected material. As the Introduction notes, for instance, seven witnesses testified to Oswald's presence at the killing of Officer Tippit, but only two of them can be quoted at length in a book of this size. The careful researcher, of course, will have to turn to the complete Government version.

Anthony Lewis' introduction adequately explains the nature of the hearings and of this selection. He endorses the Commission's fairness and competence, noting that it "analyzed every issue in exhaustive, almost archaeological detail . . . Every critical event was re-enacted. Witnesses here and abroad testified to the most obscure points."

Lewis' view must now be read in conjunction with the impressive claim of Epstein, who declares in *Inquest* that the Commission sought a "political truth." But Lewis is kinder with the doubters than are most writers, stating: "Some skepticism is understandable; it is so hard to accept unreasoning providence as the author of such deeds." But beyond the mere skeptics, he notes that those devising elaborately constructed conspiracy theories will profit from the fact that it is impossible to prove the negative—i.e., to prove that there was no conspiracy. He stresses, however, that the Commission "went to great lengths to examine all such theories and unanimously found them without substance."

Of interest to the reader will be the questioning done by Arlen Spector, Assistant Counsel to the Commission, who is credited with having developed the "single bullet hypothesis," by which a single bullet exited from the President's neck and then struck Governor Connally.

For the official, complete version, see next entry.

President's Commission on the Assassination of President Kennedy. *Hearings.* 26 Vols. Washington, D.C.: U.S. Government Printing Office, 1964.

This is the full official version of the entry cited above.

On November 29, 1963, President Johnson appointed a presidential commission headed by Chief Justice Earl Warren "to ascertain, evaluate and report upon facts relating to the assassination of the late President John Fitzgerald Kennedy and the subsequent violent death of the man charged with the assassination." The Commission began taking testimony on February 3, 1964, subsequently took testimony from 552 witnesses, accepted more than 3,000 exhibits as evidence, and on November 23, 1964, published, along with a summary *Report,* 17,000 pages of testimony and exhibits contained in 26 volumes. The first 15 volumes contain testimony and some exhibits. Volumes 16 to 26 contain exhibits only. The Commission provided no central index to its published materials. Later one was provided by Sylvia Maegher, cited in the next entry. However, each volume is provided with a table of contents and Volume 15 contains a name index. Volume 26 contains a complete list of Commission Exhibits.

Meagher, Sylvia. *Subject Index to the Warren Report and Hearings and Exhibits.* New York: Scarecrow Press, 1966. 150 pp.

This subject index to "all elements in the assassination and subsequent crimes as well as the background and history of the principals" as contained in the material published by the President's Commission on the Assassination of President Kennedy generally compensates for the lack of adequate indexing by the Commission. Miss Maegher even during this compilation was convinced that the Commission was wrong, negligent, and confused, if not worse, about many points, and steady use of the index might reveal some bias connected with these preconceptions. However, a careful examination of it indicates that it is a most welcome and useful tool for researchers of whatever degree of objectivity or kind of bias.

Anyone wishing, for instance, to determine the adequacy of the Commission's investigation of the important points of the setting and publication of the President's travel route in Dallas need only look under the entry "motorcade route" for the page numbers of all testimony, exhibits, and commentary on this subject contained in the Hearings, Report, and Exhibits published by the Commission.

Preserving "Evidence Pertaining to The Assassination of President Kennedy," *Report of the U.S. House of Representatives Committee on the Judiciary,* August 19, 1965, to accompany H.R. 9545, 6 pp. 89th Congress, 1st Session, House Report No. 813.

Only those interested in detailed research will wish to examine the background of the preservation of evidence as intended by a Congressional Committee.

Scobey, Alfredda, "A Lawyer's Notes on the Warren Commission Report," *American Bar Association Journal,* January, 1965, pp. 39–43.

A lawyer discusses the problems which would be faced by an attorney defending Oswald and his possible lines of approach in challenging the Warren Commission testimony. The differences between the Commission and a regular court are explained.

"Symposium on the Warren Commission Report," *New York Law Review,* May 1965, pp. 404–524.

A group of law professors and lawyers examine the achievements and some of the criticisms of the Warren Commission. Professor Robert Cushman's perceptive article is one of the few contributions which raises serious questions about the constitutionality of the Commission and the consequences of a Chief Justice of the United States lending his name and services to it.

Cohen Jacob, "The Vital Documents: What the Warren Commission Omits," *The Nation,* June 11, 1966, pp. 43–49.

While researching for a book in defense of the Warren Commission, this historian-lecturer ran up against the puzzling problems of some missing documents, particularly one set of autopsy photographs turned over to the Secret Service, and another which had gone to Dr. George C. Burkley, the White House physician. He describes the difficulty experienced by a defender of the Commission in obtaining answers for an adequate intellectual defense.

Greenberg, Bradley S. and Parker, Edwin B., eds. *The Kennedy Assassination and the American Public: Social Communication in Crisis.* Stanford, California: Stanford University Press, 1965. 392 pp.

A collection of articles and brief studies by newsmen, psychologists, political scientists, and communications researchers, who report on how the public heard about the assassination, how they reacted at first and later, and what their reactions were in relation to their political beliefs. Almost all of the authors are competent in their respective fields, but they seldom ask probing questions. The subject is undoubtedly important, but this treatment seems thin and at times quite pretentious. The chapter concerning social research on the assassination does not suggest more pertinent analysis; nevertheless, some of the public opinon findings cited are surprising and interesting.

DOUBTS CONCERNING THE WARREN REPORT

Jones, Penn. *Forgive My Grief.* Midlothian, Texas: *Midlothian Mirror,* 1963. Vol. 1. 188 pp.

What is distinctive about this critique of the Warren Report by this editor of a newspaper of a small town near Dallas is his remorseless collection of information about a disconcerting number of deaths of persons in one way or another connected with the tragedy in Dallas. Relating many of these deaths (for instance a part-time Dallasology sleuth Dorothy Kilgallen) to a sinister plot seems far fetched, but Jones points out that untoward events in the lives of a large number of persons connected with the Dallas story is far greater than actuarial tables would allow for and he continues to make his point, somewhat to the embarrassment of less sensational critics of the Warren Commission. If nothing more, this is at least an interesting illustration of one bizarre and jarring event becoming associated in some persons minds with subsequent bizarre events, all of which contributes to an air of unreality. A summary article drawn from this material appeared in the magazine *Ramparts,* November, 1966.

Buchanan, Thomas G. *Who Killed Kennedy?* New York: G. P. Putnam's Sons, 1964. 207 pp.

Although this is the most poorly written book to doubt the official version of the Dallas assassination, it had more impact in Europe and other continents than any of the other books on the assassination. If various agencies of American government hurt their case by prematurely releasing their conclusions, Buchanan weakened the case for doubt by rushing forth with an indictment of the Warren Commission's work before its *Report* could be carefully evaluated.

The basic thesis of the book was first published by *l'Express,* a Paris journal which had commissioned Buchanan to go to Dallas to report on the trial of Jack Ruby. *Who Killed Kennedy?* was first published in book form by Secker and Warburg of London in early March, 1964. Its author, born and educated in the United States, was for six years a correspondent for a number of European and Asian newspapers. At the time of publication of the American edition of this book, Buchanan was a resident of Paris working for a management consultant firm.

The book will live in history, if for no other reason than it received a seven page review by the FBI and became forever a part of the Warren Commission's work as Exhibit 2585. Buchanan in March of 1964 presented the major part of the British version of his book to the Warren Commission, which had the FBI check out the claims made within. Internal evidence in the book suggests that its American version was rushed to print about the time of the release of the *Warren Commission Report,* with a sketchy but pointed nine-page analysis of the report added.

Unlike Mark Lane and Joachim Joesten, Buchanan concludes that Oswald was implicated in the assassination but he concludes Oswald was only an accomplice. Buchanan's strongest point is his challenge to the theory of a single bullet striking both Kennedy and Connally. His argument stirs some suspicion of police behavior at the time of the assassination, but his accusations of right-wing oil interests being behind a plot against Kennedy seems irresponsible and seems to rest only on his left-wing attitude toward these interests. The arguments of the book are so weakly constructed that little would have come of any of them without the later, careful investigations of Edward Jay Epstein.

Joesten, Joachim. Oswald, *Assassin or Fall Guy?* Paperback, New York: Marzani, Munsell, 1964. 204 pp.

Joesten is a cosmopolitan writer from Europe who has written on espionage and counter-espionage, and who wrote, in German, a book on Kennedy's 1960 campaign. Like Lane—to whom his sentiments seem closest—and Sauvage, he doubts the guilt of Oswald. His research in Dallas and his study of news reports led him to question whether the events in that city at the time of the assassination could have happened in the time sequences ascribed to them. An approximately fifty-page analysis of the *Warren Report,* previously published as a supplement to the book, is included in the edition cited.

A weakness of his book, for many readers, will be his contention that "If no more than half of the facts, testimony and speculations in this book are true, the Oswald case is America's Dreyfus Case." Readers do not feel confident in examining a book about which its author is willing to concede so much. Nevertheless, if doubts about Dallas prove well founded, one can safely say that the left-oriented press of Marzani, Munsell kept the story alive until the prestige publishing houses had made up their minds to take it up.

The book is ill-tempered, poorly written, and lightly casts accusations with inadequate evidence, in the manner of a big talker in a neighborhood saloon. Most critics of the Commission *Report* such as Lane and Weisberg avoid citing a specific alternative explanation of the President's murder, but Joesten states flatly "I tend to the belief of a conspiracy of powerful men with a narrow circle of complicity in the middle echelons of the FBI and Dallas police."

Joesten has also published in London three related books: *Oswald: The Truth, Marina Oswald,* and *The Garrison Inquiry,* all published in London by Peter Dawnay.

Fox, Sylvan. *Unanswered Questions about President Kennedy's Assassination.* Paperback Original, New York: Award Books, 1965. 221 pp.

The question about the official version of the Dallas slaying raised by Fox's widely distributed paperback seem to have spurred a number of other skeptics to continue their research. Fox's critique may have been the result of his job as city editor of the late *New York World Telegram and Sun,* a paper where the deep press room doubts about the government version of Dallas kept popping into print much more frequently than in other papers. See Richard Starnes' "Warren Report is Big, But So Is Loophole," November 25, 1964, and Robert Ruark's "Puzzled by Warren Report," October 9, 1964 (both pieces in the *World Telegram*). Ruark, who knew his guns, wrote: "I have read the Report scrupulously several times and the ballistics end of it makes no sense."

Macdonald, Dwight, "A Critique of the Warren Report," *Esquire,* March, 1965.

Literary and political critic Macdonald is trenchantly critical of the mental outlook of the Commission and of some of their methods, but he concludes that the body of inquiry nevertheless amassed enough evidence to justify their conclusions. John Sparrow, who has emerged as a major critic of the critics of the *Report* applies praise to Macdonald's piece which more properly is due to Sparrow's own essay. Sparrow calls this article by Macdonald "the shrewdest, fairest, weightiest, and most entertaining of all the strictures on the *Report* that have been published." For the comment of another observer, this one a Yale law professor, who is quite critical of aspects of the Commission's work, but who accepts its essential conclusions see Alexander M. Bickel, "The Failure of the Warren Report," *Commentary,* October, 1966.

Epstein, Edward Jay. *Inquest: The Warren Commission and the Establishment of Truth.* Introduction by Richard Rovere. New York: Viking, 1966. 224 pp. Paperback ed., New York: Bantam Books, 1966. 193 pp.

Although several books had questioned the *Warren Commission Report,* this was the first one to be taken seriously by Establishment figures. That part of Epstein's case exposing hasty and sloppy operations on the part of the Commission seems likely to stand. Part of the book suggesting that there must have been a second assassin will have to await further disclosure of evidence for confirmation.

This book grew out of a Master's thesis done at Cornell University under the direction of Professor Andrew Hacker. Epstein realized that the Commission was not a formal court, but he was still disturbed that there was no division of function between investigator, attorney, judge, and jury. The book relies heavily on interviews of members of the Commission (not Chief Justice Warren) and ten of the twenty-seven persons on the Commission staff. Some documents from the National Archives which were not previously available are studied.

Although all of the internal memoranda and reports of agencies to the Commission have not been declassified, two FBI reports of December 3, 1963 and January 13, 1964, were made available to Epstein. These mention a bullet which entered the President's back from the rear and did not exit, which leaves the front neck wound unaccounted for. Epstein contends that various evidence in the report indicates the FBI report was correct. Because of a firing time factor established by an actual film of the murder, the lone assassin theory of the Commission Report depends upon a single bullet having entered Kennedy's back, exited from his throat, and having then struck Governor John Connally. Epstein concludes that this did not happen. He is satisfied with the evidence the Commission developed indicating Oswald was an assassin, but his evidence suggests there may have been another assassin responsible for the neck wound. He does not speculate about a conspiracy. The photos of the Bethesda Naval Hospital autopsy which were turned over to Secret Service Agent Roy Kellerman might throw further light on the question of whether there was a path through which the bullet passed from the back to exit through the throat.

Since it was always possible that these FBI reports might be made public, it is peculiar that the Warren Commission, which took pains to correct even minor mis-statements, did not in its report explain why the FBI reports conflicted with the version of the autopsy the Commission endorsed. Staff members of the Commission have merely reported that they discarded the FBI reports because their own evidence was more direct and superior. But these reports have found their way into the arguments of other doubters of the official assassination version including Weisberg and Sauvage, as well as in Philadelphia attorney Vincent Salandria's article in *The Minority of One,* April, 1966.

Epstein, it should be noted, maintains that even if these FBI reports should be disproved, he has still produced other evidence to refute the theory that a single bullet hit both Kennedy and Governor Connally.

Whatever the fate of the "single bullet theory," Epstein has made a powerful case that the Commission was unduly anxious to establish an acceptable political truth.

The influence of this sober book is indicated by the fact that it produced many serious reviews. It even caused writer Max Lerner to admit that reading it for the first time shook his faith in the *Warren Commission Report* (*New York Post,* June 26, 1966) and it caused former Kennedy aide Richard Goodwin to call for an impartial panel to review the Warren Commission's work (*Bookweek,* July 24, 1966).

Epstein's *Inquest* carried weight, but did not go without challenge. In Britain, Professor A. L. Goodhart in an article entitled "The Mysteries of the Kennedy Assassination and the English Press," *Law Quarterly Review,* January, 1967, quotes from some staff members of the Warren Commission whose interviews are important to Epstein's argument, who have informed Goodhart that they challenge Epstein's quotations and interpretations of their testimony. Furthermore, John Sparrow, cited elsewhere in this section of the bibliography, not only endorses Goodhart's objections to Epstein's research methods but employs logical analysis to challenge some of Epstein's conclusions.

Lane, Mark. *Rush to Judgment. A Critique of the Warren Commission's Inquiry into the Murders of President John F. Ken-*

nedy, Officer J. D. Tippit and Lee Harvey Oswald. New York: Holt, Rinehart and Winston, 1966. 478 pp.

This attorney and New York City political reformer drew some criticism when he pioneered in doubting the official version of the Dallas killing and held public meetings at which collections were taken. He has now put the result of his research and interviews into book form so that his critics will have to do their homework before dismissing his claims as those of a grandstander. Lane has done rather extensive interviewing in Dallas and, in addition to finding the usual logical faults in the *Warren Commission Report,* attempts to suggest alternative explanations to those of the Commission. Lane examines in detail the established and alleged relation between Jack Ruby and the Dallas police. Because his work is not as tightly reasoned as Epstein's and because he has more interest in speculation, his work will probably not have as much impact as did *Inquest.* An early report on Lane's problems when interviewing in Dallas is found in Mark Lane, "Oswald Case: Lane in Dallas," *National Guardian,* Jan. 9, 1964. His "Brief for Oswald" had appeared in the same weekly, December 19, 1964. See also Mark Lane, *A Citizen's Dissent.* Holt, Rinehart and Winston, 1968.

Popkin, Richard H. *The Second Oswald.* **Introduced by Murray Kempton. New York: Avon, paperbound, 1966. 174 pp.**

The Chairman of the Department of Philosophy of the University of California became fascinated with one of the more peculiar aspects of the assassination—the numerous reports of the appearance of a person who looked like Lee Oswald in places or circumstances where the known Lee Oswald could not have been. Popkin, along with Joesten, is a critic of the Commission Report who offers a positive alternative explanation. It is that there were two assassins—neither of them Lee Harvey Oswald. Lee Oswald's role was to be the prime suspect chased by police. The other person who had impersonated Oswald was one of the assassins. As John Sparrow, cited elsewhere in this bibliography, has pointed out, the Popkin conjecture ignores too much other evidence to be wholly credible.

Sauvage, Leo. *The Oswald Affair: An Examination of the Contradictions and Omissions of the Warren Report.* **Cleveland: World Publishing Company, 1966, 418 pp.**

Sauvage has in mind a parallel between an American Establishment conspiracy to pin the entire blame for Kennedy's assassination on Oswald and "l'affaire Dreyfus." In the earlier case, a French establishment "railroaded" Dreyfus, not because they believed him guilty, but because it was convenient to resolve certain problems that way. This respected writer, who for eighteen years has covered America for the substantial French newspaper *Le Figaro,* brings to his argument French training in logic gained at the Sorbonne and the Faculty of Law of the University of Paris. Sauvage jumped the gun somewhat by publishing a piece on "The Oswald Affair" in *Commentary,* March, 1964, only to find some of his questions answered by the *Warren Commission Report* for which he could not apparently wait. But since that report, he still finds many questions unanswered and deeply disturbing to any thinking person. He shares the concern of Epstein and others that the police and the Warren Commission did not follow all useful lines of inquiry but he departs from Epstein as well as Buchanan in maintaining that there is insufficient evidence even to prove that Oswald was one of the assassins. The reader will have to read background conditions Sauvage refers to in his book when he concludes:

> Given these conditions and bearing in mind that after the assassination, nothing was done to apprehend the guilty or to collect and save clues, or to examine or follow through the various lines of interesting possibilities—it is logically unsound, judicially indefensible and morally inadmissible to affirm that Lee Oswald was the assassin of President Kennedy.

Weisberg, Harold. *Whitewash: The Report of the Warren Commission.* Paperback Original, Hyattstown, Maryland: Harold Weisberg, 1966. 208 pp.

Harold Weisberg, a former employee of the Senate Civil Liberties Committee, severely attacks the procedures, evidence, and reporting of the Warren Commission.

Weisberg has done further research which has in part been incorporated into the case of District Attorney Jim Garrison of New Orleans charging conspiracy to assassinate President Kennedy. For reference to Weisberg's book *Oswald in New Orleans: Case for Con-*

spiracy with the CIA, see entry in this section under Roberts, Gene, "The Case of Jim Garrison and Lee Oswald."

Roberts, Gene, "The Case of Jim Garrison and Lee Oswald," *New York Times Magazine,* **May 21, 1967, pp. 32–35 ff.**

A fair and balanced evaluation of thinking in New Orleans regarding District Attorney Jim Garrison and his case charging conspiracy to assassinate President John F. Kennedy. Garrison's political instincts, past actions, and psychological make up cause some thoughtful persons to doubt his judgment in this case, but few doubt his seriousness, toughness, or legal ability.

The Garrison charge of conspiracy and related legal actions fills columns of references in the *New York Times Index* over a long span of time and the story is likely to develop for months or years before a definite literary comment on it can be written. In literary form what can be known is that much of the material Garrison considered in developing his theories and his case is contained in Harold Weisberg's *Oswald in New Orleans: Case for Conspiracy with the CIA.* New York: Canyon Books, 1967. 404 pp. Paperbound. Jim Garrison wrote the introduction to the Weisberg book, pp. 7–14.

The significance of the Garrison case was that contrary to the purely investigatory procedure of the Warren Commission, regular judicial procedures, including cross-examination of witnesses, would be used in sifting evidence relating to the assassination.

See also "Garrison, on TV, Answers Critics," *New York Times,* July 17, 1967.

Meagher, Sylvia. *Accessories After the Fact. The Warren Commission, The Authorities, and the Report.* **New York: Bobbs-Merrill Co., 1968. 477 pp.**

Miss Maegher is conceded, even by her critics, to have combed through the Warren Report volumes probably as thoroughly as anyone. She did so partly to compile an index useful to those of any persuasion or degree of objectivity who wish to analyze the work of the Commission. She has here brought together all the unexplained aspects or possible inconsistencies or omissions in the product of the Commission. Two problems detract from the study. She began with the strongest suspicions of the Commission and its members, and she lacks an analytical mind with a necessary sense of priority.

Sparrow, John, "After the Assassination," *The Times Literary Supplement,* December 14, 1967, pp. 1217–1222.

This is a serious and forceful attempt to refute the major published critics of the Warren Commission *Report*. The general command of cool logic and common sense displayed by the author, warden of All Souls College, Oxford, goes a long way toward demolishing the "demonic" conjectures of some of the Commission's critics, at the same time failing to make the reader believe the Warren Report. This 18,000-word article treats particularly the works of Mark Lane, Edward J. Epstein, Joachim Joesten, Richard H. Popkin, Harold Weisberg, Josiah Thompson, and Sylvia Meagher. Since this major critique came from so prestigious a scholar, appeared in so important a literary review, and originated from a land where passions on this subject are thought to run less high than in America, this article was greeted by some in the United States (see *New York Times,* December 14, 1967, p. 34) as an almost definite vindication of the Warren Commission Report.

Sparrow, except for branding some of his opponents as dupes, seldom loses his dispassionate stance, except, for example, when he says of Oswald: "He ran like the little rat he was." Upholders of the Warren Commission Report, like Sparrow and Manchester, make far harsher judgments of Oswald and are far more certain of his motivation than was the Commission.

Despite significant blemishes, this is the almost indispensable critical guide a fair-minded reader would wish to have on hand when reading attacks on the Warren Commission Report. This piece is also published in book form by Chilmark and distributed by Random House, New York, 1968.

Thompson, Josiah. *Six Seconds in Dallas. A Micro Study of the Kennedy Assassination.* New York: Bernard Geis Associates. Distributed by Random House, 1967. 323 pp.

Professor Thompson, who teaches philosophy at Haverford, carefully analyses physical scientific evidence relating to the moment of the assassination. Particularly, he focuses on the movements of persons in the President's car at that moment, using the movie film of Abraham Zapruder. Through deductions supported by impressive evidence he concludes that there must have been more than one gunman involved in the assassination. But as Thompson's critics point out, his conclusions conflict with other impressive evidence provided by witnesses, and Thompson has been unable to reconcile these conflicts. (See John Sparrow, cited elsewhere and Fred Graham's review of Thompson's book in *The New York Times Book Review,* February 17, 1968.) A Thompson article derived from this book, and supported by at least one other piece run in that magazine, induced the editors of *Saturday Evening Post* to join the editors of *Life* in calling for a new investigation of the assassination. Fred Graham who reviews many related books for *The New York Times* insisted that such an investigation could "do no more than inspire another round of critical books."

CHAPTER IX.

Further Research and the Kennedy Library

FURTHER RESEARCH

For most research, the above selected and annotated works, along with the indexes in the works themselves, will probably suffice. To pursue a special topic further, I suggest the researcher should inspect the following works: *The Biographic Index, Reader's Guide to Periodical Literature, Public Affairs Information Service Index, International Index,* and *The New York Times Index.* For various reviewers' evaluations of books listed in this bibliography, see *Book Review Digest* and *Book Review Index.*

An extensive list of Kennedy references available in the Library of Congress is found in the U.S. Library of Congress's General Reference and Bibliographical Division and the Bibliographical and Reference Section: *John Fitzgerald Kennedy, 1917–1963, a Chronological List of References,* Washington, D.C., U.S.G.P.O., 1964. 68 pp.

Only those doing exhaustive research on topics such as Kennedy's views on labor or foreign policy would find it worthwhile to trace Professor Burns' steps by referring to the index of the *Congressional Record* during Kennedy's years in Congress and the index of hearings published by the House Committee on Labor and Education and the

170 THE KENNEDY LITERATURE

Senate Committees on Foreign Relations, on Labor and Public Welfare and Government Operations, during years Kennedy was a member of those committees.

THE NATIONAL ARCHIVES AND RECORDS SERVICE

The National Archives, located at 8th Street and Pennsylvania Avenue, Washington, D.C., administers all presidential libraries and has now been given title to the Kennedy Library as well. The Archives, along with the Kennedy Library and the Library of Congress will be one of the great centers for Kennedy material. In addition to other presidential documents and files the Archives houses some 1,500 documents of the Warren Commission many of them available for researchers, but some still classified. Persons desiring to examine records must obtain a card of admission from the Central Reference Staff. The Archives makes available a pamphlet entitled *Regulations for the Public Use of Records in the National Archives.* See also entry under Presidency, this bibliography, by Graff, Henry F., "Preserving the Secrets of the White House," *New York Times Magazine,* December 29, 1963, pp. 9 ff., and entry under *Report of the Warren Commission.*

THE KENNEDY LIBRARY

Both for serious research as well as for more general educational purposes, the Kennedy Library in Cambridge, Massachusetts, is destined to become a mecca for students of the Kennedy Presidency. For the same reason, I have included the statement issued by the Kennedy Library describing its contents and purposes.

> The John Fitzgerald Kennedy Library will be erected in Boston, Massachusetts, at a site along the Charles River donated by Harvard University. President Kennedy personally chose this site both because he wished the Library to be close to the scenes of his own youth and because he wanted to be a part of a living educational community. The location will not only permit close relationship with Harvard University but will be within easy access of other colleges and universities in the Boston area.
> The Library will be a memorial to President Kennedy. It will

seek to express in architecture the spirit and style of the thirty-fifth President. But it will be much more than a monument; for an appropriate memorial must also express President Kennedy's vivid concern for the unfinished business of his country and the world. The Library will therefore include, in addition to an austere and beautiful Memorial room, several working components: A Museum; an Archive; and an Institute. The challenge to the architect will be to combine these elements in a single harmonious design which will both contain the various functions of the Library and celebrate the memory of President Kennedy.

The Museum will display memorabilia of President Kennedy and his times—photographs, panoramas, scientific objects, and artifacts of all sorts arranged to portray and convey the issues, the achievements and the atmosphere of the Kennedy years. The Museum will not be simply a static exhibition of items in glass cases. It will employ the modern resources of electronics and design to engage the spectator in active participation and to give the exhibits a living impact. Thus there might be a room where individuals can enter a booth, select a Kennedy speech or a significant episode of his times, and then see a film or hear a tape of the actual event. The goal of the Museum will be to make the experience of recent history as direct and intense as possible for the visitor, and especially for students and young people.

The Archive will house the personal papers of President Kennedy, his family, and his associates, as well as copies of the public records necessary to an understanding of the issues and actions of his Administration, and transcripts of interviews with his colleagues and contemporaries. In addition, there will be a collection of books, magazines, newspapers and printed documents bearing upon President Kennedy and his times. The Archive will hopefully become a center for the study of mid-century America, its basic problems in domestic and foreign policy, its conception of itself and its destiny. It will contain the necessary facilities for scholarly research, including study rooms and the most advanced equipment for a continuing oral history project, for documentary reproduction, for the use of microfilm and for the full exploitation of audiovisual materials.

The Institute will seek to further one of President Kennedy's deepest concerns—his continuing attempt to bring together the world of ideas and the world of affairs, the world of scholarship and the world of decision, as, for example, these worlds existed together in the early days of the American Republic. No purpose more consistently animated his life, and no cause could better serve his memory. The Institute will be under the direction of a man who combined scholarly eminence with practical experience in public affairs. Its object will be to enlist young Americans and young people everywhere in the understanding and practice of democratic political life and public service. It will be a living institution, responsive to the needs of the times, and its resources and programs will therefore not be rigidly committed in advance; but it can be assumed that it will strive to bring intellectual and public affairs closer together in a diversity of ways—through lectures and seminars by professors, politicians and public servants of all parties and from foreign countries as well as from the United States; through professional chairs, perhaps in joint appointment with Harvard and neighboring universities; through meeting rooms for undergraduates interested in politics and public affairs; through fellowships for students and scholars, American and foreign; through visitors-in-residence; through organization of study groups and conferences bringing together scholars and practitioners to consider vital issues; through a publication program; through literary and public service awards; and through a variety of other means. The Institute will be committed to no program or policy but only to President Kennedy's own spirit of free and rational inquiry.

Among the specific materials useful to students of the Kennedy literature which will be made available at the Kennedy Library are an annotated version of *A Thousand Days,* the biography of Kennedy by Arthur Schlesinger, Jr., material used by William Manchester in writing *The Death of a President,* interviews with major American and foreign political figures who knew, worked with, or conferred with President Kennedy. Major television networks have contributed more than 650,000 feet of news film and TV tape of Kennedy for use in the library.

President Kennedy toured Cambridge, Massachusetts looking for a library sight in the spring of 1962 when he had reason to believe he would achieve a record meriting such a monument. In any event a home town library had come to be something an American President wants and expects. After the President's tragic death generous private and business contributions were received for the library but it was nevertheless 1968 before the Massachussetts legislature appropriated the better part of $7.4 million required for the purchase of the land on Boyleston Street and Memorial Drive, Cambridge, where the library is to be located. Thus the move toward a functioning library has gone forward somewhat slowly. Kennedy had been fully aware that special presidential libraries located outside Washington, D.C., had come in for criticism as too dispersed and expensive. In fact it is estimated that some fifteen presidential libraries around the country now cost well over $1.5 million a year to maintain. Kennedy countered this by insisting these separate libraries stimulated special interest in American history and politics.

President Kennedy's press conference reply to this question, December 12, 1962 gave him an opportunity to expand on this theme and cited here gives him the last word in this bibliography:

> Q. Mr. President, your speaking of historians induces me to ask you this: most former Presidents have put their official papers in libraries in their home States, where they are not readily available to scholars and historians who come here to work with the Library of Congress and other agencies here. Have you decided where to put yours and would you consider putting it in Washington?
>
> THE PRESIDENT: Yes, I am going to put it in Cambridge, Mass. [Laughter]
> Let me say I know that we have a library now in Independence, Hyde Park, Mr. Hoover's library at Stanford, Mr. Eisenhower's library at Abilene. There are advantages and disadvantages. In some ways it helps stimulate scholarship in those areas; in addition, through scientific means of reproduction, microfilms, and all of the rest, it's possible to make documents available generally here in Washington, and through the Archives, the Library of Congress, and at the libraries. The number of scholars who deal with these subjects in detail, it seems to me, will find it possible in a central place to get the kind of documents that they need. So that while there is a problem, as you suggest, I think that we can, and this will certainly be increased as time goes on, we will find it possible to so reproduce the key documents that they will be commonly available, I would hope, in Washington. There are a great many other advantages to a library—if you've gone to Franklin Roosevelt's library and to Harry Truman's library. It offers a good deal of stimulus to the study of American history, besides being a place where you can keep for a long time documents. There are many other things of interest which I think are rather advantageous to have spread around the country, particularly as it stimulates the study of the Presidency.

Index

A

Abel, Elie, *The Missile Crisis*, 116
Alsop, Stewart, "White House Insiders," 107
Amory, Cleveland, *The Proper Bostonians*, 25

B

Bailey, T. A., "Johnson and Kennedy: The Two Thousand Days," 141
Baker, Bobby, 12-13
Baker, Leonard, *The Johnson Eclipse: A President's Vice-Presidency*, 116
Baldwin, Hanson, 14; "Managed News—Our Peacetime Censorship," 15
Blagden, Ralph M., "Cabot Lodge's Toughest Fight," 94
Blough, Roger Miles, "My Side of the Steel Price Story, As Told to Eleanor Harris," 125
Blum, J. M., 42; "Kennedy's Ten Foot Shelf," 106
Bowles, Chester, 58, 59
Bradlee, Benjamin, *That Special Grace*, 3, 144
Buchan, John (Lord Tweedmuir), 25, 43
Buchanan, Thomas G., *Who Killed Kennedy?* 158
Bundy, McGeorge, 47, 79, 118; "The President and the Peace," 112
Burns, James MacGregor, 20, 29, 32, 48, 49, 53; *John Kennedy: A Political Profile*, 75-77, 93; "Kennedy's First Year," 105; "The Four Kennedys of the First Year," 130; "The Legacy of the 1,000 Days," 133

C

"Can the Catholic Vote Swing an Election?" U.S. News and World Report, 94
Carleton, William Graves, 4, 43; "The Cult of Personality Comes

Carleton, William Graves (*cont.*) to the White House," 107; "Kennedy in History: An Early Appraisal," 138
Cater, Douglass, *Power in Washington*, 109
Chamberlain, John, "The Chameleon Image of John F. Kennedy," 93
Churchill, Sir Winston, 53
Cohen, Jacob, "The Vital Documents: What the Warren Commission Omits," 157
Collins, Frederic W., "The Mind of John F. Kennedy," 84
Congress and Nation 1945–1965: A Review of Government and Politics in the Post War Years, Congressional Quarterly, 112
Cornwell, Elmer E. Jr., *Presidential Leadership of Public Opinion*, 113
Corry, John., *The Manchester Affair*, 146
Cox, Archibald, 38
Crown, James Tracy, and Penty, George P., *Kennedy in Power*, 103; "President Kennedy—As the World Knew Him," 112; *American Government*, 174
Cushing, Cardinal, 19, 90, 91

D

Dinneen, Joseph, *The Kennedy Family*, 81-82; Joseph Kennedy Interview, 12
Donovan, Robert J., *PT 109: John F. Kennedy in World War II*, 84
Drummond, Roscoe, 48
Dulles, John Foster, 58
Dungan, Ralph, 38
Dunning, John L., "The Kennedy Assassination as Viewed by the Communist Media," 144

E

Eisenhower, Dwight D., 15, 21, 24, 35
Epstein, Edward Jay, 10; "Manchester Unexpurgated: From 'Death of Lancer' to 'Death of a President,'" 146; *Inquest: The Warren Commission and the Establishment of Truth*, 161
Evans, Rowland, and Novak, Robert, *Lyndon B. Johnson: The Exercise of Power*, 117

F

Fairlie, Henry, 4; "He Was a Man of Only One Season," 139
Falk, S. L., *The National Security Council Under Truman, Eisenhower, and Kennedy*, 113
Fay, Paul B. Jr., *The Pleasure of His Company*, 91
Fox, Sylvan, *Unanswered Questions about President Kennedy's Assassination*, 160
Fritchey, Clayton, "A Tale of One City and Two Men," 118
Frost, Robert, 41
Fuchs, Laurence, *John F. Kennedy and American Catholicism*, 126
Fuller, Helen, *Year of Trial*, vii

G

Galbraith, John Kenneth, 59, 80
Garraty, John A., *The Nature of Biography*, 11
Gavin, General James, *War and Peace in the Space Age*, 39
Golden, Harry, *Mr. Kennedy and the Negroes*, 125
Graff, Henry F., "Preserving the Secrets of the White House," 109

INDEX 177

Gray, Charles H., "A Scale Analysis of the Voting Records of Senators Kennedy, Johnson, and Goldwater, 1957–1960," 100

Greenberg, Bradley S. and Parker, Edwin B., eds., *The Kennedy Assassination and the American Public: Social Communication in Crisis*, 157

H

Hagan, Roger, "Between Two Eras," 136

Haggerty, Press Secretary James, 15

Halpern, Dr. Milton, New York City's Chief Medical Examiner, 19

Harlech, Lord (Sir David Ormsby-Gore), 28

Harper's Magazine, 23, 33, 60

Harris, Seymour F., *The Economics of the Kennedy Years and a Look Ahead*, 111; "Kennedy as Target," "Kennedy and the Intellectuals," 130

Healy, Paul F., "The Senate's Gay Young Bachelor," 81

Hearst, William Randolph, 30

Heller, Deane and David, *Jacqueline Kennedy*, 88

Henry, Laurin L., "The Transition: The New Administration," 103

Hersey, John, "Survival," 83

Hilsman, Roger, *To Move a Nation: The Politics of Foreign Policy in the Administration of John F. Kennedy*," 118

Holcombe, Arthur, "John F. Kennedy '40 as Presidential Cabinet Maker," 85

Hoopes, Roy, *What the President Does All Day*, 108

Hoover, Herbert, 21

J

Jacobson, Harold K. and Stein, Eric, *Diplomats, Scientists, and Politicians: The U.S. and the Nuclear Test Ban Negotiations*, 117

Johnson, Lyndon B., 4, 17, 110

Johnson, Samuel, 5

Jones, Penn, *Forgive My Grief*, 158

K

Kazin, Alfred, "The President and Other Intellectuals," 129

Kempton, Murray, 20, 58; "Looking Back on the Anniversary," 125

Kennedy family: Edward, 12, 18; Jacqueline, 21, 89-90; Joseph P., 24, 53, 89-90

"Kennedy Legend and the Johnson Performance," *Time*, 140

Kennedy Library, 170

"A Kennedy Runs for Congress," *Look*, 92

Kennedy Writings, 22-29, 31, 32, 38-39; *America the Beautiful*, 62; "Books in the News," 59; *The Burden and the Glory*, 31, 61-62; "The Challenge of Political Courage," 32; "A Democrat Looks at Foreign Policy," 57; "Democrat Says Party Must Lead or Get Left," 57; "The Floor Beneath Wages is Gone," 38, 65; *Inaugural Address*, 36, 39, 44; "The Intellectual and the Politician," 40; *Kennedy and the Press: The News Conferences*, 114; *John F. Kennedy on Israel*, 126; "A Message to You from the White House," 57; "My Brother Joe," in *As We Remember Joe*, 21, 30, 51; *A Nation of*

Kennedy Writings (*continued*)
Immigrants, 63; *Profiles in Courage,* 20, 21, 22, 29, 31-34, 55; *The Strategy of Peace,* 38, 59-60; "Take the Academies Out of Politics," 38; *To Turn the Tide,* 16, 21, 60-61; "The Voter's Choice in the Bay State," 58; "War in Indochina," 54-55, 65; "What My Illness Taught Me," 37; "What Should the U.S. Do in Indochina?" 38, 65; "What's Wrong With Social Security?" 38, 65; *Why England Slept,* 21, 29, 31, 38, 39, 52-54. *See also* Other published writings
Khrushchev, 16, 57, 141
Kimball, Penn, *Bobby Kennedy and the New Politics,* 121
Kluckholn, Frank L., *America Listen! An Up to the Minute Report on the Chaos in Today's Washington,* 131
Knebel, Fletcher, "Pulitzer Prize Entry: John F. Kennedy," 96; "Democratic Forecast: A Catholic in 1960," 123
Knoll, Edwin. *See* McGaffin, William, 15
Koenig, Louis, *The Chief Executive,* 110
Kraft, Joseph, 10, 18-20; *Profiles in Power: A Washington Insight,* 117
Kraus, Sidney, *The Great Debates: Background, Perspective, Effects,* 98
Krock, Arthur, 4, 14, 15, 29, 32, 33, 48, 89; "Kennedy at 46," 132

L

Lane, Mark, *Rush to Judgment,* 162

Lasky, Victor, 11, 47, 76; *John F. Kennedy: What's Behind the Image?* 96; *JFK: The Man and the Myth,* 134
Lasswell, Harold D., *Power and Personality,* 11
Levin, Prof. Murray B., 12
Liang, Margaret, *The Next Kennedy,* 12
Lincoln, Evelyn, 9, 17, 37, 46, 49; *My Twelve Years With John F. Kennedy,* 80; *Kennedy and Johnson,* 119
Lippman, Walter, *Conversations With Walter Lippman,* 140; "The Legend Reappraised," 141
Lodge, Henry Cabot Jr., 58, 94
Lowe, Jacques, *Portrait: The Emergence of John F. Kennedy,* 84; *The Kennedy Years,* 90
Luce, Henry, 30, 48
Lyons, Louis M., 16

M

Macdonald, Dwight, "A Critique of the Warren Report," 160
Mahajani, Usha, "Kennedy and the Strategy of Aid: The Clay Report and After," 115
Mailer, Norman, 41; *The Presidential Papers,* 134
Manchester, William, 12; *Portrait of a President: John F. Kennedy in Profile,* 87-88; *The Death of a President,* 144
Markel, Lester, "Management of the News—Our Peacetime Censorship," 15
McCarthy, Joseph, 33, 76
McConnell, Grant, *Steel and the Presidency,* 124
McGaffin, William, and Knoll, Erwin, *Anything But the Truth:*

INDEX

The Credibility Gap—How the News is Managed in Washington, 15
Meagher, Sylvia, *Subject Index to the Warren Report and Hearings and Exhibits,* 156; *Accessories After the Fact. The Warren Commission, the Authorities, and the Report,* 165
"Meany, Kennedy Discuss the 1960 Election Issues," *American Federationist,* 124
Meyer, Karl, 14
Meyers, Joan, *John Fitzgerald Kennedy As We Remember Him,* vii
Mollenhoff, Clark R., 16
Muggeridge, Malcolm, 4, 13; "Books," 140; "Kennedy the Man and Myth," 140

N

National Archives, 170
Neustadt, Richard E., *Presidential Power,* 101; "Approaches to Staffing the Presidency: Notes on FDR and JFK," 108; *Statement of Richard Neustadt, Professor of Government,* 113; "Kennedy in the Presidency: A Premature Appraisal," 135
Nevins, Allan, 59, 62
Newton, J. V. Jr., 16
Nixon, Richard M., 97; *Six Crises,* 98, 131
Novak, Robert and Evans, Rowland, *Lyndon B. Johnson: The Exercise of Power,* 117

O

O'Connor, Edwin, *All in the Family,* 17-18
Opotowski, Stan, *The Kennedy Government,* vii

Osborne, John, "The Economics of the Candidates," 94
Otten, Alan, *The Kennedy Circle,* 35

P

Parker, Edwin B. *See* Greenberg, Bradley.
Pearson, Drew, "Jackie's Crackdown on the JFK Books," 12, 34
Penty, George P. and Crown, James Tracy, *Kennedy in Power,* 103
Phillips, Cabell, 20, 32; "Case History of a Senate Race," 94
Popkin, Richard H., *The Second Oswald,* 163
Powell, James Grant, *An Analytical and Comparative Study of the Persuasion of Kennedy and Nixon in the 1960 Campaign,* 99
President's Commission on the Assassination of President Kennedy, *Hearings,* 155

R

Ransom, Harry Howe, *Can Democracy Survive the Cold War?* 15
Rayburn, Sam, "The Speaker Speaks of Presidents," 128
Reedy, Father John L., 86
"The Richest President, How Much He Has, How Much He Gets," *U.S. News and World Report,* 85
Roberts, Gene, "The Case of Jim Garrison and Lee Oswald," 165
Rockefeller, Nelson, 29
"Role of Robert Kennedy; No. 2 Man in Washington," *U.S. News and World Report,* 106
Roosevelt, Eleanor, "On My Own," 127
Roosevelt, Franklin, viii, 24, 42, 78-79

Ross, Irwin, "The Men Around Kennedy," 102
Rostow, W. W., 42, 59
Rovere, Richard, 128, "Letter From Washington," 15
Rukeyser, Merryle Stanley, *The Kennedy Recession*, 132
Rusk, Dean, 58, 80, 118

S

Salinger, Pierre, 17; *With Kennedy*, 91
Saltonstall, Sen. Leverett, 29, 58
Samuelson, Paul, 42
Sanghvi, Ramesh, *John F. Kennedy: A Political Biography*, 106
Sargent, H., "Versailles on the Potomac: A Report to the Bourgeoisie," 88
Saunders, Doris, *The Kennedy Years and the Negro: A Photographic Record*, 126
Sauvage, Leo, *The Oswald Affair: An Examination of the Contradictions and Omissions of the Warren Report*, 163
Schlesinger, Arthur M. Jr., 4, 9, 13, 14, 20, 32, 40, 44, 46, 49, 50; *A Thousand Days: John F. Kennedy in the White House*, 79-80; *Kennedy or Nixon; Does It Make Any Difference?* 96
Schnapper, B. N., *New Frontiers of the Kennedy Administration: Texts of the Task Force Reports Prepared for the President*, 105
Schreiber, G. R., *The Bobby Baker Affair*, 110. See also Baker, Bobby.
Scobey, Alfredda, "A Lawyer's Notes on the Warren Commission Report," 156
"The Senate's Gay Young Bachelor." See Healy, Paul F.

Settle, Trudy S., *The Faith of John F. Kennedy*, 90-91
Sevareid, Eric, *Candidates, 1960*, 33, 96
Shannon, William, 10, 20; "The Kennedy Administration: The Early Month," 128
Shaw, Mark, *The John F. Kennedys, A Family Album*, 88
Sidey, Hugh, *John F. Kennedy, President*, 48, 88
Smith, David S., *Alfred E. Smith and John Kennedy: The Religious Issue During the Presidential Campaigns of 1928 and 1960*, 99
Sorenson, Theodore, 4, 9, 11, 13, 17, 20, 32-38, 45, 46, 49-50, 59, 77; *Kennedy*, 77-79; *Decision-Making in the White House*, 108
Sparrow, John, "After the Assassination," 166
Speeches, Remarks, and Press Conferences of Senator John F. Kennedy and Vice President Richard M. Nixon, U.S. Congress, 97-98
Stevenson, Adlai, 21, 42, 58, 80, 94
Sylvester, Arthur, 14
"Symposium on the Warren Commission Report," New York Law Review, 157

T

Taft, 29, 32
Taylor, General, 42. See also General Gavin.
Thompson, Josiah, *Six Seconds in Dallas, A Micro Study of the Kennedy Assassination*, 166
Timmisch, Nick, and Johnson, William, *Robert Kennedy at 40*, 91
The Torch is Passed: The Associ-

ated Press Story of the Death of a President, 143
Truman, 24, 35
Turnbull, John W., "The Clergy Faces Mr. Kennedy," 95

U

"Union Leaders Size Up Kennedy and Johnson," *U.S. News and World Report,* 124

V

Vanocur, Sander, "Humphrey v. Kennedy: High Stakes in Wisconsin," 93

W

Warren, Chief Justice, 19
Warren Commission Report, 147
Weeks, Edward, 32, 140
Weeks, Sinclair, 58
West, Richard, 21
Whalen, Richard J., *The Founding Father: The Story of Joseph P. Kennedy and the Family he Raised to Power,* 89-90
White, Theodore, *The Making of the President,* 97
Wicker, Tom, "Kennedy as a Public Speakah," 99; *JFK and LBJ: The Influence of Personality in Politics,* 120
Wicklin, John, "Protestant and Catholic Votes Found to Offset Each Other in Kennedy's Victory," 95
Wiggins, J. R., 16
Wilson, Woodrow, 20, 23
The Witnesses: The Highlights of Hearings Before the Warren Commission On the Assassination of President Kennedy, 154

Biographical Note on James Tracy Crown

James Tracy Crown, Professor of Political Science and chairman of the Department of Politics of University College, New York University, has closely observed John F. Kennedy and the Kennedy literature since the late President entered the Senate in 1953. He has had articles on the Kennedy Administration published in the *Nation* and in *Coronet* Magazine, and he is coauthor, with George P. Penty, of *Kennedy in Power,* a paperback published by Ballantine in 1961. Biographer James MacGregor Burns reviewed this book in the *Nation,* calling it "the best analysis we shall have for some time of the anatomy of the Kennedy policies." Since his doctoral thesis on the growth of executive powers in the United States, Professor Crown has studied the office of Chief Executive and the impact of the office on the nation. He is also the author of *American Government,* published by Doubleday and Co. in 1963; his work stresses the growth and consequences of Presidential leadership. In addition, he is the editor of the Political Science section in *Good Reading,* a Mentor Books paperback, and has written the foreword to Henry A. Zeiger's *Lyndon B. Johnson, Man and President,* published by Popular Library in 1963. He is a member of the American Political Association and the International Political Science Association. He has lectured on the Kennedy Administration at American, European, and Asian universities.